KU-429-156

MODERN LEGAL STUDIES

MORTGAGES

AUSTRALIA
The Law Book Company Ltd.
Sydney : Melbourne : Brisbane

CANADA AND U.S.A.
The Carswell Company Ltd.
Agincourt, Ontario

INDIA
N. M. Tripathi Private Ltd.
Bombay

ISRAEL
Steimatzky's Agency Ltd.
Jerusalem : Tel Aviv : Haifa

MALAYSIA : SINGAPORE : BRUNEI
Malayan Law Journal (Pte.) Ltd.
Singapore

NEW ZEALAND
Sweet & Maxwell (N.Z.) Ltd.
Wellington

PAKISTAN
Pakistan Law House
Karachi

MODERN LEGAL STUDIES

MORTGAGES

by

PAUL B. FAIREST, M.A., LL.B. (Cantab.)

Professor of Law at the University of Hull
Formerly Fellow and Tutor of Selwyn College, Cambridge and University Lecturer in the Faculty of Law, Cambridge

SWEET & MAXWELL
1975

Published in 1975 by
Sweet & Maxwell Limited of
11 New Fetter Lane, London
and printed in Great Britain
by Northumberland Press Limited
Gateshead, Co. Durham

SBN Hardback 421 17810 8
Paperback 421 17820 5

CONTENTS

OTHER BOOKS IN THE SERIES:

Human Rights and Europe, by R. Beddard
Economic Torts, by D. Heydon
Registered Land, by D. Hayton
Natural Justice, by P. Jackson
Settlements of Land, by B. Harvey
Administrative Procedures, by G. Ganz
Law Reform and the Law Commission, by J. Farrar
Industrial Tribunals, by K. Whitesides and G. Hawker
Variation of Trusts, by J. Harris

GENERAL PREFACE TO MODERN LEGAL STUDIES

MODERN LEGAL STUDIES is a series written for students of law in Universities, Polytechnics, and other institutions of higher education. It originated in the belief that law students need a series of short, scholarly monographs in different areas of the law, resembling those now being produced in other fields of social science.

The Series has five principal aims. First, it aims to supplement traditional textbooks by providing opportunity both for new topics to be written about and introduced into the syllabus of traditional courses, and for older topics to be given deeper consideration than they receive in the standard texts. Secondly, as the series progresses, it aims to provide a possible alternative to the one-textbook-per-course approach of many law courses; a set of several short books in, for instance, Property Law, could be used as substitutes for the present all-purpose texts. This would enable the student to become acquainted with a variety of views and approaches to the subject. Thirdly, the existence of a series of small, relatively cheap, legal monographs will, it is hoped, facilitate the breaking of boundaries between traditional courses—*e.g.* Contract and Tort,—and the creation of new courses built upon monographs in the Series.

Fourthly, the Series aims to promote greater consideration on the part of other social scientists of the legal aspects of social political and economic problems who are too often discouraged from considering the law on a whole range of matters because of the daunting nature of legal textbooks. Without compromising on the standards of legal scholarship, a smaller monograph should prove less formidable and therefore more useable. Fifthly, and by no means least in importance, the Series offers an outlet to legal scholars in the United Kingdom and elsewhere. The Editorial Board hopes that, where they have something worth saying to a wider audience than their own students, but which does not fit the length of either a law review article or a full-length book, they will be stimulated to prepare a monograph for the Series.

Modern Legal Studies then has ambitious aims, which will be realised only with time. But it is very much a co-operative venture, between the authors, who have written or are writing for the Series, the Editorial Board, and the wider community of legal scholars, teachers and students who are both the consumers now and, it is hoped, the producers of the future.

J. P. W. B. McAuslan
University of Warwick

PREFACE

THIS book is a modest attempt to provide an outline of the modern law of mortgages of land. It is intended primarily for the use of students reading Land Law and it is assumed throughout that the reader has an understanding of the basic concepts of land law and of the elements of the system of registration of title under the Land Registration Act 1925.

The book is not intended in any way to supplant the standard treatises on mortgages, such as *Fisher and Lightwood*, or *Waldock*. It is rather an attempt to present a picture of the modern mortgage relationship, with particular emphasis on those areas of the law where modern conditions have led to continuing development. For instance, special emphasis has been placed on the mortgagee's powers of entry into possession and sale, where extensive changes in the law have occurred in the past few years. At one time, I was sorely tempted to omit all discussion of priority of mortgagees, as being of no practical importance today, but the claims of tradition were paramount, and cases such as *Barclays Bank Ltd.* v. *Taylor* and *McCarthy & Stone* v. *Hodge* showed that there was life in the old dog yet. I have tried, nevertheless, to reduce the amount of space allocated to this topic.

My main concern was for students reading law, and, for this reason, mortgages of property other than land have received scanty attention. The whole field of financing of chattel-purchase has been changed by the Consumer Credit Act 1974, which was published at a date too late for inclusion. In general, I have endeavoured to state the law as from sources available at June 1, 1974.

To many friends, colleagues, and students my debt is immeasurable. In particular, I am most grateful to Professor

J. P. W. B. McAuslan of the University of Warwick (the General Editor of the Series in which this book appears) and Professor W. R. Cornish of the London School of Economics, for reading the manuscript through in draft and for making many helpful and constructive suggestions. The burden of preparing the tables of cases and statutes was kindly undertaken by the publishers whose patience passeth all understanding. Responsibility for all errors remains, of course, my own.

December 2, 1974.

PAUL FAIREST
University of Hull

TABLE OF CASES

TABLE OF STATUTES

Chapter 1

INTRODUCTION: THE NATURE OF A MORTGAGE

In essence, a mortgage is a transfer of an interest in property as security for a loan. A mortgagee (*i.e.* one who lends money by way of mortgage) has a considerable advantage over an ordinary (or unsecured) creditor; his chances of recovering his loan do not depend entirely upon the solvency of the debtor. He has the right to recover his loan by realising the mortgaged property. He is thus not merely left to his personal remedy against the borrower; he has rights against an item of his property also, and, if he is careful to restrict the amount of his loan to the value of the mortgaged property, he will normally be able to recover his loan without undue difficulty. This process is particularly helpful when the property which is taken as security for the loan is of a permanent kind, like land. Land has tended to appreciate in value over recent decades, and thus it is particularly suitable for transactions of this kind. It is usual, for instance, for Building Societies, and other institutional lenders to lend relatively large sums of money to borrowers of relatively modest means, and to accept repayment over a relatively lengthy period—often in excess of thirty years. The investment, as far as the lender is concerned, is hardly hazardous; with the present trend in prices of land, the value of the land is likely to increase, and so afford to the lender an even greater degree of security with the passage of time.

This willingness—of Building Societies and other institutional lenders—to lend relatively large sums of money to private individuals over a long period of time has led, in the past half-century, to a very rapid increase in owner-occupation of houses, and a decline in the amount of privately rented housing. During the same period, many changes in the law have been made to provide a measure of security of tenure for the private tenant, since it was felt that in the prevailing conditions of a housing shortage the traditional attitude of freedom of contract worked to the disadvantage of the private tenant who needed a roof over his head and was thus in a weak bargaining position. As will be seen, though the legal relationship of mortgagor and mortgagee is rather different from that of landlord and tenant, the operation of the housing market, and the growth of owner-occupation, seems to be beginning to lead to the growth of similar "protective" legislation, to protect the mortgagor in the occupation of his home. The fact that there is so little legislation of this kind already is itself a tribute to the efficiency and probity of the Building Society movement; the Building Societies, and other institutional lenders, are usually willing to show a considerable amount of indulgence to a borrower who falls temporarily into difficulties, and have not taken unfair advantage of the power which they possess in a time of housing shortage. At the time of writing, there is a proposal for legislation to control certain aspects of the "second mortgage" transaction; details are not yet known, but it seems likely that the legislation will deal with matters such as advertising and interest rates, rather than the essence of the mortgagor-mortgagee relationship itself.

This book is mainly concerned with mortgages of land; in practice, this is the kind of mortgage most commonly encountered. At first sight, one would expect mortgages of chattels to be equally prominent in the modern world. After all, it is a familiar feature of modern life that such articles as cars and furniture are often bought with the assistance of "finance" from a finance company; the transaction does not appear so very different from the purchase of a house with the aid of "finance" from a Building Society or local authority. Why then, is this not an aspect of the law of mortgages too? The reason lies in the fact that in the nineteenth century, to prevent a then prevalent social abuse, the Bills of Sale Act 1878 was passed. This proved to be unsatisfactory, as the lender too easily secured priority over other creditors, and draconian enforcement of the security was still possible. Hence the 1882 Bills of Sale (Amendment) Act was passed, which had the general effect of making void all mortgages of chattels unless an extremely cumbersome list of formalities was observed. The rules are so complex that a considerable amount of space would be needed to given an account of them; but they are of very little importance in practice, since the financing of the purchase of chattels has developed by a totally different route, largely invented to escape the Bills of Sale Acts themselves. In a typical hire-purchase transaction, the transaction takes the form of a sale of the goods by the dealer to the finance company, who then let the goods out on hire to the individual consumer, who, eventually exercises his option to purchase the goods by the payment of the last instalment. This curious procedure, which effectively masks the real nature of the transaction, is really a product of history; and there is a chance that the whole law of consumer credit with regard to the purchase of chattels will be reformed reasonably soon (see the Crowther Report, Cmnd. 4596).

Hire-purchase is, of course, a convenient transaction for the lender, since his ownership of the goods is in most cases enough to ensure priority for him over the other creditors.

Terminology

It might be helpful, at this early stage, to explain some of the traditional terminology of the law of mortgages, which often appears confusing. The borrower is known as the "mortgagor"; he is the person who transfers an interest in property as the security for the loan. The lender is known as the "mortgagee"; he is the person who provides the money and takes the interest in property as the security for the money which he has lent. In most cases, today, the mortgagee is a professional in the sense that he is in the business of lending money on mortgage. Building Societies, for instance, are societies established for the purpose of raising, by the subscription of members, a fund for making advances to members upon security by way of mortgage of land (Building Societies Act 1961, s. 1(1)). In general, the only security on which a building society may advance money is land, although they can take additional security such as a life assurance policy in connection with an advance on land (Building Societies Act 1962, s. 26(1)). In general, a building society may not advance money by way of second mortgage, unless the prior mortgage is in favour of the society making the advance (Building Societies Act 1962, s. 32—and see Wurtzburg & Mills, *Building Society Law*, 13th ed., p. 55 etc.). The document by which the rights of the mortgagee in respect of the mortgaged property are created is itself known as a "mortgage."

When the loan is paid off, and the rights of the mortgagee are lifted from the property, the mortgagor is said to "redeem" his property. It is customary, for reasons which will appear later, to refer to the mortgagor's rights during the currency of the mortgage as his "equity of redemption," or more briefly, and rather confusingly, as "the equity." This is particularly confusing as the nature of a mortgage transaction nowadays is to leave vested in the mortgagor not a mere *equitable* right, but a *legal estate*, subject of course to the rights of the mortgagee. Some of these curious expressions are comprehensible only in the light of the history of mortgages, and it is to that that we must now turn.

History of Mortgages

This subject has been dealt with at length elsewhere (see, *e.g.* Megarry and Wade, *The Law of Real Property*, 3rd ed., pp. 881-886, Cheshire, *Modern Real Property*, 11th ed., pp. 621-626, Holdsworth, *History of English Law*, Vol. iii, p. 128, Simpson, *Historical Introduction to the Land Law*,) and it is not proposed to go into detail here. It is, however, clear that even a modern mortgage, and particularly some of its terminology, can only be understood in the light of the history of mortgages. The situation is particularly complicated by the differing views of the mortgage transaction taken by the Courts of Common Law and the Courts of Equity.

(a) Mortgages at Common law

The Common Law took a simple, straightforward, and robust view of the mortgage. For technical reasons, connected with the old forms of action, the mortgagee would only have an adequate security if he took a legal estate of freehold in possession in the land. Accordingly, a mortgage took the form of an outright conveyance of the fee simple to the mortgagee, as security for the loan. To distinguish the mortgage however, from an outright conveyance on sale, it was usual to insert a "proviso for reconveyance" in the mortgage. This was a stipulation that at some fixed time in the future, the loan would be repaid and the mortgagee would reconvey the legal fee simple back to the mortgagor. This date, on which the loan was to be repaid and the fee simple conveyed back to the mortgagor was known as the *legal date for redemption.*

In accordance with their normal approach to time stipulations, the courts of common law took a stern view of the terms of the mortgage. They held that the mortgagor was entitled to request reconveyance if, *but only if*, the sum lent was repaid on or before the legal date for redemption. If, on the legal date for redemption, the mortgagor was unable to pay the sum due, the common law courts regarded his right to redeem as lost and gone for ever. The legal fee simple had, of course, been vested in the mortgagee by the mortgage, subject to the proviso for reconveyance. Now the proviso for reconveyance became inoperative, and so the legal fee simple remained vested in the mortgagee absolutely, no longer subject to the proviso for reconveyance. If the mortgagor was able and willing to repay the loan at a later date, he could no longer insist on redemption.

A further complication arose from the fact that the courts of common law would not enforce the right of redemption against the land itself. True, on repayment of the loan the mortgagor had the right to demand reconveyance of the land from the mortgagee; but his right was regarded as a purely personal right, enforceable by a personal action against the mortgagee himself, and not by a real action against the land. Thus, during the mortgage, the mortgagor's rights were in essence reduced to personal rights against the mortgagee; if the mortgagee failed to reconvey on the legal date for redemption, the sole remedy of the mortgagor was to bring a personal action against the mortgagee for a breach of his covenant to repay, and the only remedy lay in damages, and not in the recovery of the land itself.

(b) The intervention of equity

The mortgage of land was an obvious case for equitable intervention. The form of a common law mortgage—an outright conveyance to the mortgagee—masked the real nature of the transaction which was that of a transfer as security for a loan. In addition, in the nature of things, the bargaining power of the mortgagor and mortgagee was not equal; an impoverished mortgagor, because of his need for funds, might be compelled to enter into an unfair transaction at the behest of a grasping mortgagee.

Equity came to the rescue of the mortgagor in two ways. First of all, a court of Equity was willing to grant specific performance of the obligation to reconvey on the tender of repayment; the borrower's right to redeem became more than a merely personal right against the mortgagee himself, but a right to recover the land itself, enforceable by an action *in rem*. The mortgagor was no longer left to his inadequate remedy in damages.

Secondly, and more importantly, the whole nature of the right to redeem, and the mortgage transaction itself, was changed by Equity. Equity looked at the substance of the transaction rather than the form, and recognised that the nature of the mortgage was a transfer as *security for a loan*. In other words, Equity regarded it as adequate if the mortgagee was given the rights as a security holder only and not as an owner of the fee simple. The mortgagee was regarded as having rights in the mortgaged property, but only such rights as could be regarded as necessary for the purpose of maintaining and protecting the security for the loan. Equity thus began to look upon the borrower in a different way. At common law, he was no longer entitled to any estate in the land, since he had transferred his estate to the mortgagee by the mortgage; Equity, on the other hand regarded him as still the owner of the property, subject, of course, to the rights of the mortgagee which Equity regarded as necessary for him to enforce his security. The borrower's rights in the mortgaged property were known as his "equity of redemption" and were freely transferable. Thus, the borrower could transfer the land to a third party; the third party would of course take the land subject to the rights of the mortgagee, but the process was known as a transfer of the equity of redemption.

As mentioned above, we still refer to the mortgagor's rights as his "equity of redemption." The terminology is no longer technically accurate, since, as we shall see, a mortgagor now retains his legal estate in possession, and the mortgagee takes not a fee simple, but some lesser estate in the land. Tradition, however, dies hard, and the expression "equity of redemption" is a convenient term to describe the ownership of land subject to a mortgage.

At the same time as these developments, Equity began to show a more tolerant attitude to a mortgagor who wished to redeem. The Common Law rule, as we have seen was a rule of "Redeem on the legal date for redemption, or not at all." Equity would allow later redemption. After all, the mortgagee only took the land as security for a loan, and if the loan was in fact repaid, together with all interest and costs, it was hard to deny redemption to a mortgagor who, maybe for some good reason, had not been able to redeem on the legal date for redemption. This *equitable right to redeem* was exercisable even after the legal date for redemption had passed, and became, in practice, a good deal more important than the legal right to redeem on the legal date for redemption. Still, like the appendix, the legal right to redeem remains in the modern mortgage as a reminder of its historical origins (see *e.g.* Hallett's *Conveyancing Precedents*, p. 606); but, unlike the appendix, it still has something of a useful function to fulfil, as it is the passing of the *legal* date for redemption which gives rise to most of the mortgagee's remedies to enforce his security. To this end, the legal date for redemption is usually arranged for a fairly short period after the creation of the mortgage; the modern mortgagor often finds, to his astonishment, that there is a clause in the mortgage which requires him to repay the mortgage loan six months after the date of the mortgage, when he had been assured by his Building Society that the mortgage was for a twenty-year term, and, of course, the mortgage also contains provisions for repayment over a twenty-year period! The purpose of the early choice of the legal date for redemption is, of course, to make the mortgagee's remedies available from an early date. It might be time now for a reappraisal of this practice; there seems to be no logical reason why a mortgagee's remedies should be tied to a legal date for redemption, as it might be thought reasonable that such remedies should stem from, and be incident to, the mortgage transaction itself.

(c) The intervention of statute

The process, begun by Equity, was continued by Statute in 1925. The property legislation of that year radically altered the form of a mortgage, and for the first time a mortgage began to reflect, in its form, its true nature. In a pre-1926 mortgage, despite the intervention of Equity, the form was always that of an outright conveyance to the mortgagee, subject only to a proviso for reconveyance on redemption; but after 1925, a mortgage began to take the form (as we shall see) of a transfer to the mortgagee of some lesser interest than the mortgagor's whole estate, either a lease or a charge. The change is basically a change in the conveyancing machinery; the protection enjoyed by the mortgagee is the same as that which he traditionally enjoyed, and his remedies are unimpaired. The legal estate is now left in the hands of the mortgagor, subject, of course, to an incumbrance to protect the security interest of the mortgagee. This incumbrance, which will bind a purchaser, will normally in practical terms inhibit the desire of the mortgagor to deal with the land as he might wish.

Parallel with this change in the legal nature of a mortgage, there has been a change in the role of the mortgage in society. In former times a mortgage was a valuable form of private investment, and the mortgage was usually secured on property which was itself an investment in the hands of the mortgagor. Nowadays private mortgagees are becoming increasingly rare; there are other, and more attractive forms of investment for the private lender, such as Unit Trusts and Property Bonds; accordingly most lending on mortgage is nowadays done by "professionals," such as Building Societies, Insurance Companies, Banks, and Finance Companies. The mortgagor is not now invariably mortgaging investment property; the property mortgaged in many cases is the mortgagor's own home, and the contribution of the institutional lenders to the growth of the movement towards owner-occupation cannot be overestimated. This trend, has, in turn, led to new problems; the traditional law of mortgages, and in particular, the law relating to the remedies of a mortgagee, does not adjust itself entirely comfortably to these changed circumstances, and many of the older authorities have to be studied in a realisation that at the time they were decided the relationship between mortgagor, mortgagee, and the mortgaged property was rather different from that prevailing today.

Chapter 2

MODERN FORMS OF MORTGAGE

One must first of all draw a distinction between legal mortgages and equitable mortgages. A legal mortgage is a mortgage which confers a *legal* interest on the mortgagee; an equitable mortgage is one which confers on the mortgagee only an *equitable* interest in the mortgaged property. The distinction holds good to some extent even in the case of registered land, where one might, in principle, expect the traditional doctrines to be less relevant.

As we shall see, in the case of unregistered land, the nature of a legal mortgage was radically changed by the 1925 legislation. The nature of an equitable mortgage underwent less modification; but such is the simplicity and convenience of the legal mortgage today that equitable mortgages are much more rarely used than was the case before 1926. Before 1926, it was, generally speaking, unusual to find the creation of successive legal mortgages, because, as we have seen, the mortgagor conveyed the whole of his fee simple to the mortgagee. Successive legal mortgages could only be created by the creation of successive terms of years (Megarry & Wade, p. 953); but since 1925, there has been no impediment to the creation of successive legal mortgages, and this has meant that the equitable mortgage has declined in practical importance (but see *infra*, p. 17). Equitable mortgages, are, generally speaking, only short-term transactions today, and are generally of a more informal nature than legal mortgages. However, they do still occur (see *McCarthy & Stone Ltd.* v. *Hodge Ltd.* [1971] 1 W.L.R. 1547) and they can cause problems, particularly with regard to questions of priority, as in *McCarthy*'s case, (*infra*, p. 42).

Legal Mortgages of Unregistered Land

Before 1926, a legal mortgage of land was affected by a conveyance of the fee simple to a mortgagee, if the land was freehold, subject to a proviso for reconveyance on redemption (*supra*, p. 5); if the land was leasehold, the mortgage took the form of an assignment of the residue of the term of years, subject to a proviso for re-assignment on redemption. This form of mortgage is no longer possible (Law of Property Act 1925, s. 85(1) (freeholds) and s. 86(1) (leaseholds)). A legal mortgage of a freehold can only now be effected by a demise for a term of years, or by a charge by deed "expressed to be by way of legal mortgage" (Law of Property Act 1925, s. 85(2)). In the case of leaseholds, a legal mortgage can now only be effected by the creation of a sub-term of years, less by one day at least than the term vested in the mortgagor, or by a similar charge expressed to be by way of legal mortgage (Law of Property Act 1925, s. 86(2)).

If a person purports to convey a fee simple, by way of mortgage, the transaction operates as a demise of the land to the mortgagee for a term of years absolute; a first mortgagee takes a term of three thousand years from the date of the mortgage, and a second mortgagee a term of three thousand years and one day and so on. This enables successive legal mortgages by demise to be created, since each mortgagee takes a term of years which will take effect in reversion to that of the mortgagee who has priority over him (Law of Property Act 1925, s. 85(2)).

In the case of leaseholds, any purported assignment by way of mortgage takes effect as a subdemise. In the case of a first mortgagee, it takes effect as a subdemise for the residue of the term vested in the mortgagor-assignor, less ten days; in like manner, second and subsequent mortgages take effect as subdemises for the residue of the term less nine days, and so on (Law of Property Act 1925, s. 86(2)).

The effect of these subsections is to ensure that any transaction which is in substance a mortgage shall take effect as a mortgage in accordance with the new procedure laid down by the Law of Property Act 1925. Their operation is illustrated by the case of *Grangeside Properties Ltd.* v. *Collingwood Securities Ltd.* [1964] 1 W.L.R. 139. In that case, a company, Eastern Trades Ltd., held a twenty-one year lease in certain premises in London, of which Grangeside Properties Ltd. were the landlords. Eastern Trades Ltd. borrowed £3,000 from Collingwoods Securities Ltd., and executed an assignment of their entire leasehold interest in favour of Collingwoods. It was conceded that although the document was in *form* an outright assignment of the lease, it was intended to operate by way of security for the loan. Subsequently, Eastern Trades Ltd. went into liquidation, and the landlords claimed that the lease was liable to forfeiture on the ground of certain breaches of covenant which had taken place. Collingwoods claimed relief against forfeiture, but they could only do so, under section 146(4) of the Law of Property Act 1925, if they were sub-lessees. They contended, successfully, that section 86(2) of the Law of Property Act 1925 operated upon the purported assignment by Eastern Trades to make it into a subdemise for the residue of the term vested in the assignor-mortgagor, less ten days. As sub-lessees under the subdemise, they were able to claim relief against forfeiture under section 146(4). In the course of his judgment, Harman L.J. observed: "[T]he Chancery would treat as a mortgage that which was intended to be a conveyance by way of security between A. and B. Once a mortgage, always a mortgage, and nothing but a mortgage has been a principle for centuries." (p. 142.)

We have seen that the Law of Property Act allowed two forms of mortgage, mortgages by demise or subdemise, and mortgages by charge. In fact, mortgages by demise or subdemise are unusual, and it is much more common to find the familiar legal charge. Such a charge creates a *legal* interest in the mortgagee (Law of Property Act 1925, s. 1(2) (*c*)); to be effective within sections 85(1) and 86(1) of the Law of Property Act, it must be by deed, and it must be "expressed to be by way of legal mortgage." In a mortgage by charge, the mortgagee takes no actual estate in the land at all, but, under section 87(1) of the Law of Property Act, he is protected in the same way as if he had a legal estate. We saw how the mortgagee in the *Grangeside* case was able to seek relief against forfeiture in the same way as a sub-lessee; in the same way, a mortgagee by charge of leasehold premises, who has no estate in the land, has been held entitled to seek relief against forfeiture as if he was a sub-lessee. In *Grand Junction Co. Ltd.* v. *Bates* [1954] 2 Q.B. 160 the plaintiff company were the freeholders of certain premises in Paddington. The tenant, a Mrs. Bates, mortgaged the premises by way of charge to Mr. Bennett. She ran the premises overtly as a guest house, but police enquiries led to her conviction for permitting the premises to be used as a brothel, contrary to a covenant in the lease. The plaintiffs then commenced forfeiture proceedings against her. She did not contest the lessor's application for possession, but Mr. Bennett, the mortgagee, did. The Court applied section 87(1) of the Law of Property Act 1925, whereby it is provided that a mortgagee by charge "shall have the same protection, powers, and remedies ... as if ... a sub-term less by one day than the term vested in the mortgagor had been created in favour of the mortgagee." This notional sub-term allowed the mortgagee to claim relief against forfeiture. (See also *Regent Oil Co. Ltd.* v. *J. A. Gregory* (*Hatch End*) *Ltd.* [1966] Ch. 402, *infra*, p. 63).

In practice, mortgages by charge are almost invariably used. They possess a number of advantages over mortgages by demise or subdemise, as they enable a mortgagor, by one document, to create a mortgage over a mixed collection of freehold and leasehold properties; in addition, the document itself is less complex and misleading. In addition, if the premises charged are leasehold, there is no risk of the mortgage itself amounting to a breach of a covenant against subletting, which is commonly found in leases. Although section 86(1) of the Law of Property Act provides that "where a licence to subdemise by way of mortgage is required, such licence shall not be unreasonably refused," most mortgagees would prefer to steer clear of the pitfalls altogether, by taking a mortgage by charge. It is possible that the enforcement of his right to possession by a mortgagee by charge will amount to a breach of covenant if the covenant prohibits the lessee from parting with possession of the property, as it commonly will; but as we shall see, the enforcement by the mortgagee of his right to possession is now considerably curtailed by Statute (*infra*, p. 53).

In Waldock's *Law of Mortgages* (1949), at p. 42, there is a spirited defence of the mortgage by charge against some antiquarians, who preferred, on the ground of "lesser obscurity" (*sic*) the mortgage by demise; it now appears to be generally thought that the battle fought by Waldock and others has been won (Report of Committee on the Enforcement of Judgment Debts (The Payne Committee) Cmnd. 3909, para. 1347). It may be doubted whether the preservation of the mortgage by demise continues to serve any useful purpose.

It will be recalled that one of the advantages of the new system of creation of legal mortgages is that it encourages the creation of successive legal mortgages of the same land. This is so whether or not the title deeds are deposited with the first mortgagee; we shall see, when we come to deal with registered land, that matters are not quite so simple in that case.

Legal Mortgages of Registered Land

In general, the provisions for creating a legal mortgage of registered land work in a similar manner to the provisions for the creation of a legal mortgage of unregistered land. Sections 85 and 86 of the Law of Property Act apply to registered land in the same way as to unregistered land (Law of Property Act 1925, ss. 85(3) and 86(3)). The usual way of creating a legal mortgage of registered land is by a deed, creating a registered charge in favour of the mortgagee, in accordance with the provisions of section 25 of the Land Registration Act 1925. The terminology hereabouts is confusing. A *charge*, properly so called, is an agreement whereby defined property is specifically made responsible for the discharge of an obligation without any transfer of possession or title to the creditor. A chargee, in the strict sense, has no right to foreclose (see *infra*, p. 72), as there is no title vested in him to enable him to foreclose. In the context of the Land Registration Act, however, the expression charge seems to have the same connotation as "mortgage", in that the registered proprietor of a charge can foreclose and exercise other remedies in the same way as a mortgagee of unregistered land.

The deed creating the charge may operate by way of demise or subdemise; (Land Registration Act, s. 27(1)); but in the absence of any provision causing the deed to take effect in this way it will take effect as a charge by way of legal mortgage (*ibid.*) In the case of registered land, as with unregistered land, it is unusual to find a mortgage operating by way of demise, as the familiar form of mortgage by way of legal charge readily lends itself to use in the case of registered land.

There is one minor difference, however, from the situation with regard to unregistered land, and one major difference. The minor difference flows from the nature of registration of title itself. The charge is only completely effective in favour of the chargee when he has been registered as the proprietor of the charge, in accordance with section 26 of the Land Registration Act, 1925. The rule is that it is registration, and registration alone, which creates the interest in favour of the chargee, and the exercise by the chargee of his powers as mortgagee is conditional upon his first procuring his registration as proprietor of the charge. In *Lever Finance* v. *Needleman's Trustee* [1956] Ch. 375 a transferee of a mortgage sought to exercise his statutory power of appointment of a receiver (*infra*, p. 75). It was held that he could not do so until he had procured his own registration as proprietor of the charge. This requirement of registration as a chargee may have an important effect on the nature of the title taken by the mortgagee. Like any purchaser of registered land, he will take subject to overriding interests subsisting *at the date of registration* (*Re Boyle's Claim* [1961] 1 W.L.R. 339), such as the "rights of every person in actual occupation of the land" (Land Registration Act 1925, s. 70(1)(*g*)). Thus if there was a tenant in occupation of the premises at the time of the chargee's registration as proprietor of the charge he will take subject to the rights of the tenant (see *infra*, p. 40) (*Grace Rymer Investments* v. *Waite* [1958] Ch. 831).

The major difference from unregistered land is as follows. In the case of unregistered land, there is no difficulty about the creation of a series of legal mortgages, even though the title deeds have been deposited with a prior equitable mortgagee. With registered land, the position is more complex. The usual procedure is for the mortgagor to surrender his land certificate to the Registry, and for the Registry to issue a Charge Certificate to the registered chargee, retaining the Land Certificate in the registry. If this has been done, there is no difficulty about the creation and registration of a series of legal charges in favour of a series of chargees. If however, of the land certificate has been deposited elsewhere, as might be the case where a prior equitable mortgage has been created, there seems to be no way in which a later legal mortgagee can become registered as the proprietor of his charge (see Hayton, *Registered Land*, p. 124). This is particularly inconvenient, for, as we have seen, a chargee cannot exercise his statutory powers until his interest has been registered.

Most legal mortgages of registered land are made by this process of registered charge. However, to complicate the issue, there appears to be another way of creating a legal mortgage of registered land. The Land Registration Act seems to be anxious to preserve some of the old methods of unregistered conveyancing, and section 106(1) of the Act provides that "The proprietor of any registered land may, subject to any entry to the contrary on the register, mortgage, by deed or otherwise, the land or any part thereof in any manner which would have been permissible if the land had not been registered, and with the like effect." This in effect makes it possible to create a legal mortgage in any way, such as by charge or by demise, as would be possible in the case of unregistered land. The Act then goes on to provide, in section 106(2), that a mortgage made under this section may, if by deed, be protected by a caution "in a specially prescribed form" and *"in no other way."* If so protected, the mortgagee may then require the mortgage to be registered as a charge (s. 106(5)), and the mortgagee will then have all the powers of the proprietor of a registered charge (s. 105(6)). Recently, this section has been the subject of some complex litigation in the case of *Barclays Bank Ltd.* v. *Taylor* [1973] 2 W.L.R. 593, which is mainly concerned with the question of a priority of a mortgage by deed not protected by special caution (see *infra*, p. 118). Suffice to say for the moment, however, that a mortgage by deed not protected by special caution is not totally ineffective, as it will prevail, at least, over a subsequent *equitable* interest, as section 106(4) seems to suggest. Section 106, in its entirety, seems to constitute a "trap for the unwary" (E. C. Ryder, (1966) 19 C.L.P. 26), and it may be regarded as doubtful whether section 106 serves any useful purpose at all. Its reconsideration, as a matter of urgency, seems desirable.

Equitable Mortgages of Unregistered Land

Here, again, the distinction between mortgages and charges becomes relevant. So far as legal mortgages and charges of registered and unregistered land are concerned, we have seen that the distinction is no longer of great moment, because a legal chargee is given by Statute (Law of Property Act 1925, s. 87, *supra*, p. 13) all the rights and remedies of a legal mortgagee by demise or subdemise. In equity, however, the distinction is still of some importance, as the rules relating to equitable mortgages are still to some extent governed by the law which prevailed before 1925, and the remedies of an equitable chargee are inferior to those of an equitable mortgagee. A mortgage is a transaction whereby an interest in property is transferred to the mortgagee as security for a loan, subject to a right of redemption vested in the mortgagor.

In a charge, the chargee is given certain rights over the property charged, but he has no right to foreclose, (*infra*, p. 72) since he has no interest in the property to enable him to do so.

Equitable mortgages are of two general types:

(i) where the mortgagor has only an equitable interest

(ii) where the mortgage is informal.

(a) Where the mortgagor holds only an equitable interest

Here, the form of a mortgage has not been altered by the 1925 legislation. The mortgage should still be effected by a conveyance of the mortgagor's whole interest to the mortgagee, subject to a proviso for reconveyance on redemption. Writing is needed, as this is a "disposition" of an equitable interest within section 53(1)(*c*) of the Law of Property Act 1925. It is desirable, though not essential, for the mortgagee to give notice to the trustees for the purpose of gaining or preserving priority under the rule in *Dearle* v. *Hall* (1828) 3 Russ. 1 (*infra*, p. 123).

(b) Informal mortgages

To create a legal mortgage, a deed is essential (Law of Property Act 1925, s. 52). In the absence of a deed, however, equity will, by analogy with the rule in *Walsh* v. *Lonsdale* ((1882) 21 Ch. 9), regard a specifically enforceable contract to create a mortgage as effective in equity to create an equitable mortgage (*Cradock* v. *Scottish Provident Institution* (1893) 69 L.T. 380 *Parker* v. *Housefield* (1834) 2 My. & K. 418, 420). It should be noted, however, that the doctrine of *Walsh* v. *Lonsdale* only applies if the contract is specifically enforceable (*cf*. in a different context, *Warmington* v. *Miller* [1973] Q.B. 877. That is to say, there must either be a note or memorandum in writing sufficient to comply with section 40 of the Law of Property Act 1925, or some sufficient act or part performance to make the contract specifically enforceable in equity (*Mounsey* v. *Rankin* (1885) Cab. & El. 496). The advancement of the money by the mortgagee to the mortgagor will not of itself amount to a sufficient act of part performance, since it is not "unequivocally referable" to some such contract as that alleged to exist (*Rogers* v. *Challis* (1859) 27 Beav. 175 but see now *Steadman* v. *Steadman* [1974] 3 W.L.R. 56).

There is one particular act, however, which has invariably been regarded as a sufficient act of part performance, and that is the deposit by the mortgagor with the mortgagee of his title deeds. The deposit of deeds is regarded as such an "unequivocal" act of part performance that a separate sub-category of equitable informal mortgage—a "mortgage by deposit of deeds" can be said to have emerged. The act of depositing the title deeds with the mortgagee is taken both as evidence of a contract to create a mortgage, and as part performance of that contract. The rule seems to be a rather anomalous extension of the normal rules of part performance, since deposit is regarded as an act of part performance by both the mortgagor and mortgagee.

To constitute an equitable mortgage, however, the deposit must have been made for the purpose of creating a security. Mere possession of the title deeds will not give the possessor the rights of a mortgagee if the depositor subsequently becomes indebted to the depositee. Thus, if a person deposits his title deeds with a bank for safe custody and subsequently overdraws his account at the bank, the bank does not acquire the rights of a mortgagee by virtue of their possession of the title deeds (*Re Beetham* (1887) 18 Q.B.D. 766).

Equitable Charges

An equitable charge is created when some specific property is appropriated to the discharge of some debt or obligation. No special form of words is required—for instance, if a written contract is signed whereby the chargor acknowledges that Blackacre stands charged with the payment of a specific sum to a creditor, this will create an equitable charge over Blackacre in favour of the chargee. Equitable charges are occasionally created, but the remedies of a chargee are inferior to those of a mortgagee, and so there is little incentive for their creation.

Equitable Mortgages of Registered Land

Here the situation is amazingly complex, as the provisions of the Land Registration Act and Rules seem to overlap in a most confusing manner.

First, there appears to be no reason why, in principle, an equitable mortgage should not achieve substantive registration as a registered charge within sections 25-36 of the Act. These sections are usually taken to apply in practice to legal charges, but there seems to be no convincing reason why equitable charges should not be accommodated within these sections also. In *Re White Rose Cottage* [1964] Ch. 483; [1965] Ch. 940, a mortgagor mortgaged some property to a bank by a species of equitable mortgage; although the point did not arise directly for decision, Wilberforce J. at first instance, was of opinion that the charge could have been protected by substantive registration under section 26 (p. 490). Lord Denning M.R., in the Court of Appeal, disagreed with this suggestion, and thought that the provisions as to substantive registration were applicable only to legal charges. With respect, the view of Wilberforce J. seems preferable; the effect of registration is laid down in section 27(1), which provides that a registered charge shall, *subject to any provision to the contrary contained in the charge*, take effect as a charge by way of legal mortgage. It has been suggested (see Ryder, (1966) 19 C.L.P. at p. 37) that the provision to the contrary contemplated by section 27(1) could take the form of a specific provision that the charge in question was to take effect in equity. So long as it was made by deed, it should still be capable of substantive registration.

Secondly, it seems that a mortgage made by deed but not protected by a special caution as section 106(2) of the Act requires for full efficacy, will take effect in equity in the meantime (s. 106(4)). *Barclays Bank Ltd.* v. *Taylor* [1973] 2 W.L.R. 293 (*infra*, p. 118).

Thirdly, a mortgage not made by deed will take effect as an equitable mortgage, if the transaction is one which would have been permissible with regard to unregistered land and with the like effect (s. 106(1)). To safeguard the rights of the mortgagee against third parties, such a mortgage should be protected by an ordinary caution against dealings (s. 54, s. 106(2)).

Fourthly, a mortgage by simple deposit of the land certificate creates, in accordance with section 66 of the Land Registration Act of 1925, "a lien on the registered land"; such lien is equivalent "to a lien created in the case of unregistered land by the deposit of documents of title." The terminology hereabouts is curious; a lien is usually a right arising by operation of law, but here a lien seems to be used in the sense of a charge. Such a lien should be protected by entry of a notice of deposit (or of intended deposit, in those cases where the transaction is intended to be completed after the issue of a land certificate), under Rule 239, which (confusingly) takes effect in the same way as a caution under section 54.

A final possibility emerges from sections 48 and 49 of the Act. Under section 48, a lessee may apply to the Registrar for registration of notice of a lease, and by section 49, these provisions are extended to certain other rights, including Land Charges (s. 49(1)(*c*)). In this way, it would seem that an ordinary puisne mortgage or general equitable charge (both of which are interests falling within the Land Charges Act, in sections 2(4)(i) and 2(4)(iii) respectively) could both be made with respect to registered land and protected by notice in accordance with section 49 (see Hayton, *Registered Land*, p. 130).

It may be doubted whether it is necessary for such complexity to exist. Section 66 would seem to create an adequate way of creating mortgages or liens of registered land, and one might think that that should do.

See also:

Megarry & Wade, *The Law of Real Property* (3rd ed.), pp. 886-898.
Cheshire, *Modern Law of Real Property* (11th ed), pp. 626-636.
Waldock, *Law of Mortgages*, pp. 19-58.
Fisher & Lightwood, *Law of Mortgages*, pp. 20-65.

CHAPTER 3

PROTECTION OF THE EQUITY OF REDEMPTION

WE have seen above that the essence of a mortgage, in the eyes of equity, is that it is a transfer of an interest in property as security for a loan of money; we have seen how equity insisted on regarding a mortgage transaction in this way despite the outward appearance of the transaction. We have seen that this is still the case; in *Grangeside Properties Ltd.* v. *Collingwoods Securities Ltd.* [1964] 1 W.L.R. 139 (*supra*, p. 12) a document which was in form an outright assignment of a lease but which was intended to operate as security for a loan was treated by the court as a mortgage so as to enable the assignee-mortgagee to claim relief against forfeiture of the lease by the head-lessor, as if the mortgagee were a sub-lessee. This case shows that the test of a mortgage is really a test of substance, not one of form. As Harman L.J. remarked, "Once a mortgage, always a mortgage, and nothing but a mortgage." (*Supra*, p. 12.)

The development of the doctrine of the equity of redemption, was, as we have seen, an intervention to preserve the substance of a mortgage transaction as a security transaction. At the same time equity has traditionally been jealous to prevent any reduction of the right to redeem by contract. Equity was always conscious that a mortgagor, at the time he was seeking his loan, might not be in a strong bargaining position *vis à vis* the mortgagee, and that the mortgagor might be compelled by considerations of financial stringency to agree to terms which might impair or impede his right to redeem. Hence the equitable doctrine grew up that there must be no "clogs or fetters" on the equity of redemption, and any that the mortgagee sought to impose upon the mortgagor would be held void, as an unwarrantable interference with the equitable right to redeem.

This doctrine of equity, however, runs counter to another hallowed doctrine of the law, that of sanctity of contract. The idea that bargains are made to be kept, not broken, lies at the foundation of commercial dealings. Many of the cases are by no means easy to reconcile because of the conflict between the two principles of "sanctity of contract" and "no clogs on the equity of redemption." Also, because of the uncertainty surrounding some of the cases on this topic, it is by no means easy to predict the way in which future cases will be decided. It seems now to be acknowledged that the doctrine of clogs and fetters on the equity of redemption is a technical doctrine, in no way connected with oppression in fact; if a given provision is held by the court to constitute a clog on the equity of redemption, it seems that it is the duty of the court to hold the provision void, even though it is clear that the provision in question is a perfectly fair and reasonable one, and which was in no way forced upon an impecunious borrower by a grasping mortgagee (see *Lewis* v. *Frank Love Ltd.* [1961] 1 W.L.R. 261; 77 L.Q.R. 163).

For the purpose of exposition it is possible to divide the cases up into three groups.

(a) Attempts to exclude redemption

The obvious way in which a mortgagee might seek to exclude the mortgagor's right to redeem, of course, is by the insertion into the mortgage of an option for the mortgagee to purchase the mortgaged property, and thus acquire the unencumbered fee simple, freed and discharged from the equity of redemption. The effect of such an option is of course to change the nature of the transaction from a transfer by way of security to what is essentially a transfer on sale, at the option of the mortgagee.

It is clear that the effect of inclusion of such an option in the mortgage itself is to render the option void, even if the transaction itself is a perfectly fair one and the price is reasonable. In *Samuel* v. *Jarrah* [1904] A.C. 323, a mortgage of some stock contained a clause giving the mortgagee the option to purchase the stock within twelve months; it was conceded that the bargain was freely entered into and the price fair. When the mortgagee sought to exercise the option, he was unable to do so as the option was held to be void by the House of Lords. The House of Lords regarded the doctrine of clogs and fetters on the equity of redemption as too well established to be disturbed, but clearly they reached their decision in the case without any particular enthusiasm for the doctrine. Lord Halsbury, in a brief but robust speech, said that the arrangement was "contrary to a principle of equity, the sense or reason of which [he was] not able to appreciate."

It will be observed that in the case of *Samuel* v. *Jarrah* the option related to the mortgaged property itself. It is less clear whether the same result would have been obtained had the option related to other property of the mortgagor. Suppose, for instance, A. mortgages Blackacre to B. and in the mortgage grants B. an option in respect of Whiteacre. The exercise by B. of the option in respect of Whiteacre does not in any way impede or fetter the redemption of Blackacre, and thus it might be argued that the option should be a valid one. However, if one looks at the *rationale* behind the doctrine of clogs and fetters on the equity of redemption—that a mortgagor seeking a loan is in a position where he is vulnerable to pressure from an unscrupulous mortgagee—it might be thought that such an option would be held void.

The judicial reluctance to upset commercial bargains between businessmen, exemplified in the speech of Lord Halsbury in *Samuel* v. *Jarrah* (*supra*) probably accounts for the willingness of the courts to distinguish the case if, for instance, the option was granted *after* the mortgage. There is, true enough, a logic in the distinction, because after the mortgagor has obtained his loan, he is no longer in a position where he is vulnerable to pressure from the mortgagee. Thus, in *Reeve* v. *Lisle* [1902] A.C. 461, the House of Lords considered an option granted to a mortgagee in respect of a steamship which had ten days previously been mortgaged to the same mortgagee. In a series of brief speeches, the House decided that the mortgage and the option were separate and independent transactions and that the option was valid.

Pausing there for a moment, one may beg leave to doubt the logic of the alleged distinction between *Samuel* v. *Jarrah* and *Reeve* v. *Lisle*. It might be supposed to rest, as we have seen, on the theory that once the mortgagor has obtained his loan he is immune from pressure, and thus there can be no objection to giving the option its full contractual validity. But is it true to say that the mortgagor is in a vulnerable position only *until* he has obtained his loan? Could it not be argued that, even after the mortgage has been granted, a mortgagor might be threatened by the mortgagee with an exercise of his powers as mortgagee, and might thus be induced to enter into a disadvantageous bargain? There is no suggestion that anything of the sort took place in *Reeve* v. *Lisle*, but caution might be needed in future cases, as *Reeve* v. *Lisle* might be used as a subterfuge to evade the rule in *Samuel* v. *Jarrah*, as, for instance, by arranging for the "option" to be dated a day later than the mortgage deed. The point would of course be irrelevant if the mortgagor was protected by the law in all circumstances against an unwarranted and oppressive exercise by the mortgagee of his powers, but, as we shall see later, this is not necessarily the case.

The Courts, then, so far, seem to regard *Samuel* v. *Jarrah* and *Reeve* v. *Lisle* as laying down clear rules of law, and they seem to have approached their task in subsequent cases as one of merely allocating the problem to one category or the other. For instance, in *Lewis* v. *Frank Love Ltd.* [1961] 1 W.L.R. 261 the plaintiff mortgaged certain property in South London to X. On X's death, his executors sought to call in the loan, and gave the plaintiff, in accordance with the terms of the mortgage, notice to repay the loan. The plaintiff then approached the defendants to see if they would be willing to take a transfer of the mortgage from X's executors, and thus step into the shoes of the deceased X as mortgagee. They were willing to accept a transfer, but only on condition that they were given an option to purchase part of the mortgaged property. The option was a fair commercial bargain, and the price was reasonable, but Plowman J. held that the case was analogous to that of *Samuel* v. *Jarrah* and thus the option was void. Presumably, if the option had been granted to X, after the first mortgage had been granted, and then X's executors had transferred both the option and the mortgage to the defendant company, the option would have been held valid in accordance with *Reeve* v. *Lisle*.

(b) Postponement of redemption

Sometimes, instead of purporting to exclude the right of redemption for all time, the mortgage may contain a clause which merely postpones the exercise of the right to redeem. In other words, the mortgagor is allowed to redeem, but only after a certain date. Here the cases are not altogether easy to reconcile. In *Fairclough* v. *Swan Brewery Co. Ltd.* [1912] A.C. 565 a mortgagor mortgaged a leasehold hotel to a Brewery Company. The mortgage contained a clause whereby the mortgagor undertook not to exercise his right to redeem for sixteen years, a mere six weeks before the expiry of the lease under which the premises were held. The Privy Council upheld a claim by the mortgagor to redeem the property at an earlier date. If the mortgagor had only been able to redeem at the date stated in the mortgage, the property, on redemption, would have been virtually worthless. The Privy Council went so far as to say that "equity will not permit any device or contrivance being part of the mortgage transaction or contemporaneous with it to prevent or impede redemption."

It was made clear, however, in a later case, that this dictum goes too far. In *Knightsbridge Estates* v. *Byrne* [1939] Ch. 441, a property company borrowed over £300,000 from the Prudential Assurance Company Limited. The advance was secured by a mortgage of certain properties in London, and the mortgage stipulated that the loan was not to be repaid before forty years had elapsed. Soon after the mortgage was granted, the property company wished to take advantage of a fall in interest rates and borrow money more cheaply elsewhere. They sought to redeem the loan before the expiry of the period stated in the mortgage. The Court of Appeal refused to allow the mortgagor's claim for early redemption. They said that the agreement was "a commercial agreement between two important companies experienced in such matters, and had none of the features of an oppressive bargain where the borrower [was] at the mercy of an unscrupulous lender." They firmly rejected the idea of "unreasonableness" of the postponement as a test; the question of the "reasonableness" of a bargain is one for the parties and their advisers, and not for the court. The real explanation, said the court, of the *Swan Brewery* case, was that the right of redemption was there rendered *illusory*; it was only in such a case that equity would interfere with a bargain. This view of the law was not directly considered by the House of Lords, to whom the case went on appeal, since they held that the transaction in question was a debenture, which by Statute, can be made irredeemable ([1940] A.C. 613, see Companies Act 1948, s. 89, replacing Companies Act 1929, s. 74).

Many cases of postponement, however, are not as simple as this. In many of the recent cases, there has been an additional factor, tying the mortgagor to sell the mortgagee's products for the duration of the loan (a "sales agreement") and preventing redemption for a period. In *Esso Petroleum Co. Ltd.* v. *Harper's Garage* (*Stourport*) *Ltd.* [1965] A.C. 269, the mortgagor had mortgaged a garage to a petrol company. The mortgagor undertook to repay the loan over a period of twenty-one years, and not to redeem before the period of twenty-one years had elapsed. He also undertook to sell only Esso petroleum products during the term of the mortgage. The mortgagor sought to redeem the mortgage before the twenty-one years had elapsed and to sell another kind of petrol. The House of Lords decided the question purely and simply as a problem of restraint of trade; having decided that restraint of trade principles were applicable to mortgages, they then held that the restraint was unreasonable in duration and so would not be enforced by the courts. The appearance of a test of reasonableness in this context, however, is not a reversal of the approach of the Court of Appeal in *Knightsbridge Estates* v. *Byrne*; it is, rather, an application of the contractual principle that an agreement which is in restraint of trade will only be enforced if it is (a) reasonable between the parties and (b) reasonable in the public interest (see *Nordenfelt* v. *Maxim Nordenfelt Guns and Ammunition Co. Ltd.* [1894] A.C. 535). Some members of the Court of Appeal appeared to be willing to hold the tie bad as a postponement of redemption, in itself, but the point was not pursued in the House of Lords.

It seems that, in this context, a postponement for a lesser period, coupled with a tie to sell only the mortgagee's products, will be valid, as in *Texaco Ltd.* v. *Mulberry Filling Station Ltd.* [1972] 1 W.L.R. 814. In *Esso* v. *Harpers* itself, the House of Lords held valid a tie for five years (unsupported by a mortgage) in respect of another garage owned by Harpers Ltd. Similarly, if the tie and the mortgage are separate and independent transactions, the tie will be held valid if it is not unreasonable in duration (as in *Re Petrol Filling Station, Vauxhall Bridge Road* (1969) P. & C.R. 1).

(c) Collateral advantages

Quite commonly, a mortgage may contain other clauses governing the relationship between the mortgagor and the mortgagee. For instance, if the parties are traders, the loan may be made between parties with a common trading interest, as between a petrol company and a garage, or a brewery and a publican. The mortgagor may, as an incident of such a mortgage, undertake to sell only the products of the mortgagee at his trade outlet. Clearly there is a risk that at the time when the mortgagor is negotiating his loan, he may be persuaded to enter into some disadvantageous trading bargain as part of the price of the loan, and the courts are ever vigilant to protect mortgagors from oppression; but at the same time, the courts are not unnaturally reluctant to disturb freely negotiated commercial bargains, arrived at by businessmen after a careful calculation of all the advantages and disadvantages implicit in such a bargain. There is some danger that a business agreement which happens to be enshrined in a mortgage might be regarded as in some mysterious way less binding than an ordinary business transaction. It cannot be said that, faced with these conflicting principles, the courts have been entirely consistent in their approach to the problems raised by the issue of "collateral advantages" in mortgages. In many cases, such as the case of *Kreglinger* v. *New Patagonia Meat and Cold Storage Company Ltd.* [1914] A.C. 25, the courts have shown an understandable reluctance to disturb a reasonable commercial agreement; at the same time, they have shown, in other cases, a willingness to come to the rescue of the improvident and oppressed (as in *Cityland Property (Holdings) Ltd.* v. *Dabrah* (*infra*, p. 32)).

In general, in so far as the "tie" purports to affect the mortgaged property and the relationship between the parties before redemption, the courts are less willing to interfere than they are in the case of a tie which purports to affect the property after redemption. For instance, in *Biggs* v. *Hoddinott* [1898] 2 Ch. 307, a clause tying the owner of a hotel to sell only the beer supplied by his mortgagee, a brewer, was held to be valid; in like manner, in *Noakes* v. *Rice* (*infra*, p. 33) it was *assumed* that such a tie, at least so far as it purported to bind the mortgagor until redemption, was valid, the real issue in that case being the continuation of the tie after redemption of the property by the mortgagor.

These cases, must, however, now be regarded as of doubtful validity, in view of the decision of the House of Lords in *Esso* v. *Harpers* (*supra*, p. 28). There it was pointed out that in the "brewer's tie" cases such as *Biggs* v. *Hoddinott* and *Noakes* v. *Rice*, the issue of restraint of trade had not been mentioned; nor had the restraint of trade issue been canvassed in the earlier petrol station case of *Hills* v. *Regent Oil Co. Ltd.* [1962] E.G.D. 452. It was only in *Esso* v.

Harpers that it was judicially recognised that mortgages of land were "within the doctrine" (see Heydon, [1969] L.Q.R. 229) and that the twin tests of "reasonableness," as enunciated in *Nordenfelt*'s case, applied to stipulations in mortgages which were prima facie in restraint of trade. Presumably, as a result of *Esso* v. *Harper*, such tying covenants in mortgages will be prima facie void, unless the party seeking to impose the tie (usually the mortgagee) can show that the covenant is not unreasonable as between the parties to the tie; such factors as the length of the tie are clearly relevant. In addition, there is the rule that although such a tie might be thought to be not unreasonable as regards the parties, it might be contrary to the public interest and so unenforceable (see Treitel, *Law of Contract*, 3rd ed., p. 395 and Cheshire & Fifoot, *Law of Contract*, 8th ed., p. 363). Indeed this ground appears to be relied upon by Lord Wilberforce himself in the course of his speech in *Esso* v. *Harpers* (at p. 340).

A further possibility arises; apart from issues of restraint of trade, a stipulation in a mortgage may be struck down on the ground that it is "oppressive and unreasonable." This, at first sight, seems surprising. Except for the restricted area of restraint of trade, where the courts have long claimed the right to adjudicate upon the reasonableness of a bargain, one might expect the courts to assume that the parties themselves are the best judges of the fairness of their transaction, and that it is not for the courts to try to remake their contracts for them. In former times, many aspects of the mortgage transaction, especially with regard to such matters as interest rates, were controlled by the Usury laws; but these were repealed in 1854 and later replaced by the modern system of statutory control of, and licensing of, moneylenders (Moneylenders Acts 1900-27). In those cases where the lender is a person who carries on the business of a moneylender, the Moneylenders Acts control the rate of interest and forbid the charging of compound interest. Most mortgagees, of course, are not moneylenders as defined by the Acts, and thus do not fall within these stipulations. Many modern mortgages do not contain a clause fixing the rate of interest;

they usually provide that the mortgagor shall pay interest at the rate from time to time in force, thus allowing the mortgagee to vary the rate of interest payable to suit the flow of money. There has been some suggestion of legislation to require the true rate of interest to be stated in advertisements published by second mortgage companies, but there has been little attempt as yet to control such matters as interest rates by legislation. It is rather surprising, therefore, to discover that in a recent case (where the mortgagee was not a money-lender) the court in effect struck down a term which provided for the payment of interest at a rate regarded by the court as oppressive.

In *Cityland and Property* (*Holdings*) *Ltd.* v. *Dabrah* [1968] Ch. 166, the defendant, Mr. Dabrah, had been the tenant for eleven years of a house of which the plaintiff company were the registered proprietors. When the tenant's lease expired in 1965, the registered proprietors sold the house to Mr. Dabrah (who became the registered proprietor) for £3,500. The purchaser paid £600 in cash, the balance of the purchase price, £2,900, being raised by means of a mortgage of the house to the plaintiff company. The mortgage was rather unusual in that it made no provision for the payment of interest on the capital sum, but the deed provided that the capital sum repayable by the defendant was to be £4,553, the extra £1,653 constituting a "premium." Had payment of this sum been spread over three years (the duration of the mortgage), it would represent interest at the rate of 19 per cent. per annum; as a proportion of the capital sum (since the whole sum was payable immediately in the event of a default) it represented interest at the rate of 57 per cent. Goff J. held that a mortgagee was entitled to only a *reasonable* sum by way of interest. The sum was fixed by the judge in the circumstances of the case as 7 per cent., although presumably a higher rate of interest would be fixed today. The term in the mortgage itself was held to be unenforceable on the ground that it was oppressive and unreasonable.

The case forms an interesting contrast in approach to that of the Court of Appeal in *Knightsbridge Estates* v. *Byrne* (*supra*, p. 27). It will be recalled that in that case the Court of Appeal laid it down emphatically that questions of reasonableness were primarily matters for the parties themselves, and that it was not for the court to impose its own standard of reasonableness. The key to the contrast may lie in the fact that in *Cityland* v. *Dabrah* there was no equality of bargaining power, and the defendant may well have agreed to the term in the mortgage in order to save himself from being rendered homeless at the expiry of his lease.

Cases concerned with ties before redemption are relatively rare; cases where an attempt has been made to impose some tie after redemption are much more common, although there is no complete consistency in the authorities. Prima facie, one might expect that any term which sought to impose a fetter on the mortgaged property after the redemption of the mortgage would be void, since a mortgagor, on redeeming his property, should be able to do as he likes with it as the mortgage is now a thing of the past. In *Noakes* v. *Rice* [1902] A.C. 24 a publican mortgaged his public house to a brewery. The mortgage contained a covenant whereby the mortgagor covenanted to sell only beer brewed by the mortgagee both during the currency of the mortgage, and after redemption. It was assumed that the tie during the currency of the mortgage was unobjectionable, although it would probably now come under scrutiny as being in restraint of trade (*supra*, p. 30); the tie after the redemption of the property was however held to be entirely void. Clearly, if such a tie were to be upheld, the mortgagor would be in a worse position after redemption than he had been before he mortgaged the property to the mortgagee. Before the mortgage the property had been a free house; the publican would in effect be getting a tied house back after redemption.

The principle of this case was extended in the later case of *Bradley* v. *Carritt* [1903] A.C. 253. In that case the mortgagor was to get his property back unimpaired, but he would be obliged to retain the property after redemption so as to enable him to comply with a tie which affected the conduct of his business. In that case, Bradley, the majority shareholder in a tea company, mortgaged his shares to Carritt, a member of a firm of tea-brokers. Since the inception of Bradley's company, Carritt's firm had acted as brokers to the company. In the mortgage, there was a covenant whereby Bradley undertook to engage Carritt's firm as brokers to his tea company thereafter. The question then arose whether, after redemption, Bradley's company were free to engage another firm of tea-brokers to act in connection with their business. It will be noticed that in fact Bradley got his shares back in their pristine condition; the shares, as shares, were in no worse state than when he had mortgaged them to Carritt. However, his dealings with the shares were circumscribed in that he would have to retain his shares so that he could use his majority shareholding to ensure that the firm of Carritt was retained as broker to the company. His shares were in effect rendered inalienable. The House of Lords by a bare majority held that the tie was invalid. Lord Macnaghten thought that it was not necessary for there to be any encumbrance upon the mortgaged property, subsisting after redemption, to bring into play the doctrine of clogs and fetters on the equity of redemption. It sufficed that the shares were enveloped in "an atmosphere of danger."

It is not easy to reconcile the case of *Bradley* v. *Carritt* with the latter case of *Kreglinger* v. *New Patagonia Meat and Cold Storage Co. Ltd.* [1914] A.C. 25. In that case the Company borrowed £10,000 from Kreglinger, secured by a floating charge over the company's assets. As a further stipulation, the Company promised to give Kreglinger, a woolbroker, a right of pre-emption in respect of all sheepskins sold by the company for the next five years. This right of pre-emption was held to be valid and enforceable, even after the floating charge had been paid off. The House of Lords appear to have distinguished their own decision in *Bradley* v. *Carritt* on the ground that the stipulation in the *Kreglinger* case was collateral to the mortgage transaction. It is not easy to see how the tie in the *Kreglinger* case could be regarded as any more collateral than the offending stipulation in the case of *Bradley* v. *Carritt*, which the court seemed to regard as "integral." In each case the clause that was the subject matter of the dispute was contained in the same document as that creating the mortgage; it would in any event be absurd if the decision in *Bradley* v. *Carritt* could be circumvented by the device of placing the offending stipulation in a separate document.

If the test is one of substance, not form, it is not easy to see how in substance the *Kreglinger* tie was any more collateral than the tie in *Bradley* v. *Carritt*. The real key to the distinction may lie in the observation by Lord Parker of Waddington in *Kreglinger*'s case that the arrangement in that case was a "perfectly fair and businesslike transaction" and Lord Mersey's comment that the arrangement was "of a most ordinary commercial kind." Lord Mersey's whole approach to the problem posed by the case may possibly be regarded as best summarised by the vigorous coda to his judgment, where he likened the doctrine of clogs and fetters on the equity of redemption to "an unruly dog, which if not securely chained to its own kennel, is prone to wander into places where it ought not to be." (p. 46.)

Is it possible for a mortgagee to impose a tie for a definite period (the expected duration of the mortgage) and then to insist upon the continuation of the tie throughout the period despite the earlier redemption of the mortgage? Can he, in other words, keep the mortgage alive in a sense (despite redemption) for the purpose of holding the mortgagor to a tie which was expected to last for the probable duration of the mortgage? In *Santley* v. *Wilde* [1899] 2 Ch. 474 the validity of such a tie seems to have been established, but the decision is open to question. In that case, the plaintiff, the tenant of the Royalty Theatre, mortgaged her interest in the theatre to Mr. Wilde for the sum of £3,000, repayable over five years. She also undertook to pay to the mortgagee, for the remainder of the duration of the lease, one third of the net profits to be obtained from underleasing the theatre, and to pay this sum even if the principal sum secured by the mortgage had been repaid. The Court of Appeal upheld the defendant's rights to a proportion of the share of the profits even after repayment of the principal sum. The decision in this case was severely criticised by the House of Lords in the later case of *Noakes* v. *Rice* (*supra*, p. 33) and its present status must be regarded as doubtful. Waldock (*Law of Mortgages* at p. 187) suggests that the decision itself can probably be supported on the totally different ground that the transaction was not essentially one of mortgage, at all, but really a partnership agreement to share the profits of the theatre.

See also:

Megarry & Wade, pp. 931-937.
Cheshire, pp. 637-646.
Waldock, pp. 175-192.
Fisher & Lightwood, p. 464.
Nokes, pp. 110-119.

CHAPTER 4

INVESTIGATION OF TITLE BY THE MORTGAGEE

IT might appear, at first sight, that there is little to be said on this subject which does not appear already in one of the standard works on Conveyancing (see *e.g.* Bowman & Tyler, *Elements of Conveyancing*; Farrand, *Contract and Conveyance*; Barnsley, *Law and Practice of Conveyancing*). Those books deal in considerable detail with the process of investigation of title by a purchaser of land. In many cases, purchase and mortgage are virtually simultaneous transactions—indeed it is often the mortgage advance which enables the purchaser to complete his purchase. The investigation of title on behalf of the purchaser and the mortgagee is often conducted at the same time, and by the same solicitor. There is no real danger of conflict here as the interests of mortgagee and purchaser are not really adverse, as they are both concerned to see that the purchaser acquires a good title which will be an acceptable security in the hands of the mortgagee. Some recent cases, however, have suggested that all might not be as simple as at first sight might appear; a mortgagee is exposed to some more serious risks than a cursory investigation might suggest.

It is assumed throughout this chapter that the reader is familiar, in outline at least, with the process of investigation of title which usually precedes a conveyance to a purchaser of the legal estate in the land. In general, of course, a mortgagee will only be bound by interests in the land which will bind the purchaser, his mortgagor. There is however, a problem. Although in practice, purchase and mortgage are simultaneous transactions, there is a moment in time—as it is sometimes called, a *scintilla temporis*—for which the mortgagor is entitled to the property unencumbered. Strange and artificial though this concept may seem, it is odd how many mortgagors have contrived to put the *scintilla temporis* to good and profitable use by the creation of an incumbrance which will bind the mortgagee! It may be observed that many of these problems spring from this curious doctrine of the *scintilla temporis*, the existence of which in no way reflects the reality of the situation; coming down to brass tacks, it is surely the mortgage advance which, in the majority of cases, enables the purchaser to complete his purchase, and to search for a moment when the purchaser is in unencumbered enjoyment of the land seems to be something of a search for living dinosaurs! It may well be that the whole notion of the *scintilla temporis*, representing, as it does, a real threat to the security of the mortgagee, should be critically examined; but there is no doubt that it is still around. Indeed, as Mr. Heydon has pointed out, it is only by some such doctrine that the decision of the House of Lords in *Esso* v. *Harpers Garage* can be reconciled with the reasoning in the case (see (1969) 86 L.Q.R., p. 233).

The types of incumbrance which can pose a threat to the mortgagee's security fall into three main classes:

(a) tenancy agreements;
(b) other contractual rights, such as an agreement to sell the fee simple;
(c) rights arising under trusts.

It is proposed to examine each of these in turn.

(a) Tenancy agreements

The main threat to the mortgagee's security here arises from the fact that the *scintilla temporis* (*i.e.* the moment in time when the mortgagor is entitled in unencumbered fee simple to the property) may suffice to create a legal tenancy by estoppel out of purported leases previously granted by the mortgagor. This legal tenancy will then be binding on the mortgagee. Thus, in *Church of England Building Society* v. *Piskor* [1954] Ch. 533, the defendant agreed to purchase a house in Croydon with the assistance of a mortgage from the plaintiff Building Society. Piskor obtained possession of the house before completion, and purported to grant weekly tenancies of part of the house to T1 and T2, who moved into the premises. At the time when he purported to grant the tenancies to T1 and T2, the legal estate was still of course vested in the vendor of the house. Some weeks later, the purchase was completed and the mortgage in favour of the Building Society executed by the defendant. Some time later, after a default by the mortgagor, the Building Society commenced proceedings to gain possession of the premises (see *infra*, p. 53). The Court of Appeal held that the mortgagee took subject to the rights of the tenants, T1 and T2. Since, of course, the tenants were protected by the Rent Acts, the mortgagee could not evict them simply by giving them notice to quit. It was held that the original leases by the mortgagor were mere leases by estoppel, since he had no interest in the land at the time of their creation out of which a legal lease could be created. It was held, however, that the legal estate vested in the mortgagor at the time of the conveyance by the vendor, and when the legal estate became so vested the leases became legal incumbrances by the feeding of the estoppel.

If the title to the land had been registered under the Land Registration Acts, a similar principle would seem to apply. The interests of the tenants could be regarded as "overriding interests" within the Land Registration Act, as they would fall either within section 70(1)(*g*) ("the rights of every person in actual occupation of the land") or within section 70(1)(*k*) ("leases for any term or interest not exceeding twenty-one years, granted at a rent without taking a fine").... Indeed, it seems that tenants could claim protection under the latter paragraph even if they had not taken possession of the demised premises, since there is no requirement in that paragraph of "actual occupation" by the incumbrancer claiming the overriding interest. It seems probable that in the case of registered land the estoppel is regarded as being "fed" by the mortgagor's acquisition of title on completion of the purchase even though, in strict theory, the legal estate does not vest in the mortgagor until registration of the transfer (Land Registration Act 1925, section 19(1)) (*Mornington Permanent Building Society* v. *Kenway* [1953] 3 Ch. 382; *Universal Permanent Building Society* v. *Cooke* [1952] Ch. 95; *Woolwich Equitable Building Society* v. *Marshall* [1952] Ch. 1 and *cf.* A. M. Prichard (1964) 80 L.Q.R. 370).

It will be observed that in these cases the mortgagor has purported to grant a *lease* to the tenant. If the transaction was a mere *agreement for a lease*, the mortgagee is in a stronger position, at least if the title to the land has not been registered under the Land Registration Act. In the case of unregistered land, the agreement for a lease will constitute an "estate contract" under the Land Charges Act 1972 (s. 2(4)(iv)), and, unless registered, it will be void against a purchaser for money or money's worth of a legal estate (Land Charges Act 1972, s. 4(6)). A "purchaser," in this context, includes a mortgagee (Land Charges Act 1972, s. 17(1)). The mortgagee will not be bound even if the "tenant" is in occupation of the premises, since a purchaser is not to be prejudicially affected by notice of rights which are registrable under the Land Charges Act but which have not been so registered. (Law of Property Act s. 199(1)(i), and *Hollington Bros. Ltd.* v. *Rhodes* [1951] 2 T.L.R. 691, 696).

In the case of registered land, however, the rights of a person holding under an agreement for a lease may constitute an overriding interest within section 70(1)(*g*) above, if the person claiming the rights is in actual occupation of the land. It seems that if the "tenant" is out of occupation, he cannot claim protection within section 70(1)(*k*) of the Act, since that paragraph deals only with leases which have actually been granted, and this has been held to exclude from protection within the paragraph a mere agreement for a lease (*Universal Permanent Building Society* v. *Cooke* (*supra*); *Grace Rymer Investments Ltd.* v. *Waite* [1958] Ch. 831 and *cf. Bridges* v. *Mees* [1957] Ch. 475, and *Webb* v. *Pollmount* [1966] Ch. 534).

These cases are of some importance in view of the general

practice of excluding, in mortgages today, the mortgagor's leasing power under section 99 of the Law of Property Act 1925 (*infra*, p. 85). It is well established that a tenancy created by a mortgagor after the exclusion of such leasing power does not bind the mortgagee, unless he has done something to "adopt" the tenancy (see *infra*, p. 86). Such a provision excluding the statutory leasing power is of no avail, however, to the mortgagee if the tenancy in question was created before the mortgage, at a time when the mortgagor was not inhibited by the exclusion of his power to grant leases. A tenancy created during the *scintilla temporis* is not caught by the provision in the mortgage excluding the leasing power (*Church of England Building Society* v. *Piskor* (*supra*)). The only circumstance in which the mortgagee can claim priority over the tenancy is if the tenant has been party to a fraudulent representation to the mortgagee that the property has not been let (the probable explanation of *Coventry Permanent Economic Building Society* v. *Jones* [1951] 1 All E.R. 901).

The melancholy but inescapable conclusion from all this seems to be that a mortgagee would be wise to check that the premises are not, in fact, let before the completion of the mortgage transaction; this might be thought to be a counsel of perfection which institutional lenders can hardly be expected to comply with. A mortgagee who finds that the property has been let by his mortgagor may have something of a long stop by reliance on the covenants for title implied in a mortgage which may give him a right of action against the mortgagor; but this will be of scant comfort in many cases, since the mortgagee will only discover the true situation on the occasion when he is seeking to exercise his remedies in respect of the security because of a default by the mortgagor. If the mortgagor is in default, any theoretical remedy which the mortgagee may be able to pursue by virtue of the covenants for title will be illusory.

(b) Contractual rights

Similarly, a contract by a mortgagor to sell the fee simple may create problems for a mortgagee. So far as unregistered land is concerned, such a contract is prima facie registrable as an estate contract within section 2(4)(iv) of the Land Charges Act 1972, and, unless it is so registered, it will be void against a purchaser for money or money's worth of the land charged therewith. This, at any rate, will enable a legal mortgagee to disregard the rights of the purchaser under the estate contract. It may, however, be binding upon an equitable mortgagee, since the unregistered charge is only declared by Statute to be void against a purchaser for money or money's worth of a *legal* estate (Land Charges Act 1972, s. 4(6)). Where the equities are equal the first in time prevails. Even where the equities are thought to be unequal (for instance, because the equitable mortgagee has subsequently acquired the legal estate) a mortgagee will be bound by an unregistered estate contract if at the time of his equitable mortgage he had actual, constructive or imputed notice thereof. Thus, in the case of *McCarthy & Stone Ltd.* v. *Hodge Ltd.* [1971] 1 W.L.R. 1547 (see [1972] A.C.L.J.), 34, an estate owning company, Cityfield Properties Ltd., agreed to sell some building land to the plaintiffs, a building and construction company, and then granted an equitable mortgage to the defendants, a firm of merchant bankers. The equitable mortgage was subsequently converted into a legal mortgage by the defendants by the exercise of a power of attorney contained in the equitable mortgage itself. When Cityfield Ltd. went into liquidation the question arose whether the mortgage took priority over the rights of the building company under their estate contract. The estate contract had not been registered at the time of the creation of the equitable mortgage, although it had been registered at the time that the mortgage was converted into a legal mortgage by the exercise of the power of attorney. It was held that the equitable mortgagees were bound by the estate contract in favour of the plaintiffs, since, at the time of the creation of the equitable mortgage the mortgagee had at least constructive notice of the estate contract, since, if he had bothered to inspect the property, he would have seen there, much in evidence, the builders and their impedimenta.

In cases where the title to the land in question is registered under the Land Registration Acts, it seems that where the person claiming rights under the estate contract is in actual occupation of the land, his rights will be binding upon a mortgagee (s. 70(1)(*g*), and see *Bridges* v. *Mees* (*supra*) and *Webb* v. *Pollmount* (*supra*)).

(c) Trusts

Here again, the law is in a state of some complexity. As far as unregistered land is concerned, the law seems to be that a mortgagee will be bound by a trust which was created before the mortgage if he has actual, constructive, or imputed notice thereof, unless the trust in question is one which can be overreached under the provisions of the Law of Property Act (s. 2) and the statutory formalities concerning the payment of capital sums that have been complied with (s. 27(2)). There appear to be two main kinds of trusts which are potentially of concern to a mortgagee in this situation. The first kind is a trust of the kind which cannot be overreached, because it does not fall within the overreaching provisions of the Law of Property Act. A bare trust—where A declares himself a trustee of Blackacre for B—would seem to fall in such a category. In *Hodgson* v. *Marks* (*infra*, p. 46) a mortgagee was held bound by a bare trust which had arisen in favour of the plaintiff. The case was in fact decided under section 70(1)(*g*) of the Land Registration Act, as the land in question was registered; but it is thought that the same result would have been achieved if the title to the land had not been registered, as the mortgagee would have been taken to have notice of the trust from the fact that the plaintiff continued to reside on the premises, and her presence would have given the mortgagee constructive notice of her rights.

The problem may also arise in connection with the more

familiar trusts for sale. In these cases the beneficial interests are capable of being overreached under section 2 of the Law of Property Act, but in many cases the overreaching machinery will not work because the statutory formalities requiring the payment of the purchase price to two trustees will not have been observed. It is not necessary to assume that this failure to comply with the statutory requirements results from any sharp practice or skullduggery on the part of the mortgagor—he may not even realise that he *is* a trustee for sale. It seems clear that in cases where the requirements of section 27(2) are not observed, the question of whether the beneficial interest binds the purchaser or the mortgagee will be treated purely as one of notice. In many cases, the question of notice will be a difficult one as the beneficiary under the trust (which is usually an implied trust) will be in occupation of the premises. The beneficiary may be in occupation together with the trustee-mortgagor, or may be in sole occupation.

These problems fell to be considered by Stamp J. in the case of *Caunce* v. *Caunce* [1969] 1 W.L.R. 286 ((1969) 33 Conv. (N.S.) 240, (J. F. Garner)). In that case a wife contributed to the purchase price of a house, of which her husband was the sole owner at law. Subsequently, the husband, without his wife's knowledge, mortgaged the house to a bank. After the husband became bankrupt, the bank commenced proceedings to enforce their security, and claimed possession of the premises. It was held by Stamp J. that the contribution to the purchase price by the wife created a trust in her favour. Since this was a case of beneficial co-ownership, there was necessarily a trust for sale (Settled Land Act 1925, s. 36(4), as interpreted in *Bull* v. *Bull* [1955] 1 Q.B. 234). The wife's beneficial interest could of course have been overreached on a mortgage by the payment of the mortgage money to two trustees, in accordance with section 27(2) of the Law of Property Act. This had not been done, as the bank had paid all the money over to the husband, believing him to be solely and beneficially entitled to the premises. The wife claimed that as she had at all times remained in occupation of the premises the bank had notice of her beneficial interest and were thus bound by it.

The learned judge rejected this argument, and held that the mortgagee was not bound by the beneficial interest of the wife. Her presence on the premises was not enough to give the bank constructive notice of her beneficial interest in the premises. She was not, said the learned judge, in "apparent" occupation of the premises, and had the bank inspected the premises and found her resident there, her presence (that of a wife in her husband's home) was totally consistent with the title which the husband had offered to the bank. To require a mortgagee to conduct an elaborate investigation into the status and possible contribution of all persons who might be resident on the mortgaged premises would be unrealistic. The judge accepted counsel's submission that it was not in the public interest that banks and mortgagees should be required to act as snoopers and busybodies in relation to wholly normal transactions of mortgage.

The case itself, which is of great importance, was concerned with the beneficial interest in favour of a wife. There may be others, however, who can lay claim to a beneficial interest in the premises arising under an implied trust by reason of a contribution (direct or indirect) or by reason of an improvement to the premises (*cf.* the claim of the mother-in-law in *Hussey* v. *Palmer* [1972] 1 W.L.R. 1286; [1973] C.L.J. 41). What would be their position if the premises had been mortgaged? Although the point was not strictly necessary to his decision, the judge in *Caunce* dealt with them too. Their presence, said the judge, would not be sufficient to give notice to a mortgagee, because the presence of such a person on the premises would not be in any way "inconsistent" with the title offered, at any rate so long as the mortgagor himself was also in possession of the premises which were the subject matter of the mortgage. "It is otherwise if [the mortgagor] is not in occupation and you find another party whose presence demands an explanation and whose presence you ignore at your peril" (p. 294).

This rule, which seems to favour mortgagees who adopt

their customary procedures (or non-procedures) on investigation of title, has, however, been severely limited in its effect by the decision of the Court of Appeal in *Hodgson* v. *Marks* [1971] Ch. 892. In that case, the title to the land in question was registered under the Land Registration Act, and the actual decision turned on the interpretation of section 70(1)(*g*) of the Act. Russell L.J., in delivering the judgment of the Court of Appeal, said (at p. 934):

> "I would only add that I do not consider it necessary to this decision to pronounce on the decision in *Caunce* v. *Caunce*. In that case the occupation of the wife may have been rightly taken to be not her occupation but that of her husband. In so far, however, as some phrases in the judgment might appear to lay down a general proposition that inquiry need not be made of any person on the premises if the proposed vendor himself appears to be in occupation, I would not accept them."

The result of this rebuff to the decision in *Caunce* v. *Caunce* appears to increase the burden of a mortgagee on investigating title. It would seem that he is now obliged to make enquiry of all persons in occupation of the premises to see if they claim a beneficial interest in the property to be mortgaged. Since beneficial interests have been found to exist in some rather unlikely persons such as mistresses and mothers-in-law, the process of enquiry is likely to be fraught with interest and excitement. Paradoxically, the only beneficiary that a mortgagee need lose no sleep about *is* a wife, if the dicta in *Hodgson* v. *Marks* are correct; but presumably enquiry must be made to see if the lady actually is a wife. Enquiry of the mortgagor himself will not suffice; he may not disclose that others have a beneficial interest, or he may not realise that they have such an interest. In *Hodgson* v. *Marks*, Russell L.J. said of the mortgagee: "As to the defendant building society, it is plain that it made no inquiries on the spot save as to repairs; it relied on [the mortgagor] who lied to it, and I waste no tears on it." The inconvenience of this rule is manifest; banks, building societies, and the like are not detective agencies, and to expect them to behave as if they were is to overlook their true function, unless, of course, the concurrence of the wife in the mortgage transaction is obtained.

In the case of unregistered land, at least, there seems to be a vestigial function for the doctrine of notice to perform. The position with regard to registered land is more uncertain, but it is probable that notice has nothing to do with the point. It is likely that beneficial interests in the land will, if the beneficiary is in actual occupation of the land, constitute "overriding interests" within section 70(1)(*g*) of the Land Registration Act 1925 and so bind a purchaser and mortgagee. It has been held that rights under a bare trust can constitute an overriding interest within section 70(1)(*g*) if the beneficiary is in occupation of the premises (*Hodgson* v. *Marks* (*supra*); *Marks* v. *Attallah* (1966) 110 S.J. 709; I.J. Leeming (1971) 35 Conv. N.S. 255). It seems but a short step from there to admit the beneficial interests arising from a trust for sale as overriding interests as well, so long as the "beneficiary" is in occupation of the premises. If beneficial interests under trusts for sale are once admitted into the select (or rather, unselect) category of overriding interests, then notice, as such, becomes irrelevant. If the interest exists, then it overrides, and that is that. The only ways of escape from this highly unpalatable conclusion come from a rigid application of the equitable doctrine of conversion, so that the rights of the beneficiaries are regarded throughout as interests in personalty and not interests in land, (but *cf. Elias* v. *Mitchell* [1972] Ch. 652) and are thus incapable of binding a purchaser or mortgagee of the land (as suggested by Mr. Hayton, in (1969) 33 Conv. (N.S.) 254), or by redefining the doctrine of notice so that only those who are in "apparent" occupation will have overriding interests. This was suggested by the trial judge in *Hodgson* v. *Marks* but did not secure approval from the Court of Appeal; Professor Maudsley has suggested that this may be the best way out of the dilemma, as has been held in certain jurisdictions in the United States ((1973) 36 M.L.R. 30).

In the Maryland case of *Crossley* v. *Hartman* (235 A. 2d 743) for instance, the Court of Appeals of Maryland held that the unexplained possession of mortgaged premises by a vendor and her nephew did not give notice of their equitable life interests in the property to a mortgagee who relied upon a paper title in the vendor, who was also in occupation of the premises. As the court said: "To hold otherwise, would, in many instances, practically destroy the effect of our registration laws."

CHAPTER 5

RIGHTS AND REMEDIES OF A MORTGAGEE

THE purpose of the rights and remedies of the mortgagee is to enable him to enforce his rights against the property in the event of a default by the mortgagor. Most of these rights and remedies are now statutory, and are contained in the Law of Property Act 1925, but the Act in general only codifies principles already established at common law. As we shall see, many of these remedies were developed at a time when a mortgage was essentially regarded as an investment by both the mortgagor and mortgagee. This is no longer the case today. The difficulty is that the traditional rights and remedies evolved in the context of investment mortgages, and for mortgages of this type are still apposite; but in many cases today the property which is the subject matter of the mortgage is the mortgagor's own home, and the traditional remedies and rights of the mortgagee have needed some re-adjustment to meet the changing social role of the mortgage. The traditional remedies have not fitted altogether happily into this new situation, and the process of development and adjustment is still continuing. In general, the courts have been vigilant to ensure that the remedies given to a mortgagee are there to protect his security, and for no other purpose; in other words, a mortgagee will in general be prevented from using his remedies to make a profit for himself. The process whereby, in the last century, the legislature has gradually extended protection to the occupiers of rented accommodation has been parallelled by a similar process whereby mortgagors are protected in the occupation of their own homes. The process has been a slow one, and is still going on; the fact that the development of protection has been so slow is itself a reflection of the probity and integrity of the institutional lenders such as building societies.

The process of erosion of a mortgagee's remedies must not be pressed too far. It is tempting to observe, of Building Societies and other institutional lenders such as Banks, that they are large and wealthy corporations and can afford to lose their security. This overlooks the fact however that building societies have to consider the interests of their depositors (many of whom are by no means affluent) and that losses by a building society can only be recouped, in the long run, by raising the rate of interest to all mortgagors.

It is a familiar feature that the institutional lenders will only advance money to a mortgagor after a fairly thorough enquiry into his means; they generally try to arrange matters so that the periodical repayments required of him are comfortably within his earnings (and those of his wife, which are now increasingly taken into account). Thus attempts are made to ensure that defaults are kept to a minimum. These attempts appear in general to be successful (see the Annual Reports of the Chief Registrar of Friendly Societies). Some problems have however arisen in connection with a loan on second mortgage. Money lent in this way is often used for improvements of various kinds to the house used as security; there is no necessary tie, however, between the loan and the purpose for which it is used—indeed many of the advertisements emphasise the borrowers freedom to spend it on anything he chooses. Some people have been led by this sort of advertising to endanger the security of their homes for the sake of some unnecessary extravagance. The Crowther Commission (pp. 263-264) have proposed a system of licensing of brokers and agents for the making of such loans and restrictions on advertising. The purpose of these proposals is to prevent some of the serious abuses which at present exist in the field of second mortgage lending, and the danger of forcing more credit on a borrower than he really wants.

It might be convenient at this point to list the various remedies which are available to a legal mortgagee faced with a defaulting mortgagor. They are cumulative, in that the mortgagee can pursue several simultaneously;

(a) action on the personal covenant to repay
(b) entry into possession
(c) sale
(d) foreclosure
(e) appointment of a receiver.

We shall deal later with other rights of a mortgagee, such as his right to possession of the title deeds, and his right to insist on consolidation by a mortgagor who is seeking to redeem.

(a) Action on the personal covenant to repay

Most mortgages contain an express provision for a covenant by the mortgagor to repay the loan. In the case of a private investment mortgage, the mortgagor generally covenants to make periodic payments of interest, and to pay off the capital sum at a given date. In the much more common type of instalment mortgage favoured by the institutional lenders, the mortgagor covenants to make a fixed payment at regular intervals, which are usually monthly. Each instalment is both a payment of interest and a repayment of part of the principal sum. At the commencement of the mortgage, each instalment consists almost entirely of interest, but as time passes, each instalment contains a larger element of principal and a lesser element of interest. Most Building Society mortgages contain a provision for alteration in the monthly instalments to take care of variations in interest rates to take account of the flow of funds into Building Societies; usually, the required instalments can be varied by the Society on giving a specified period of notice to the mortgagor. In such cases it has become traditional for the Building Societies to give the mortgagor the option if he so desires, of continuing to pay instalments at his former rate but of extending the term of the mortgage to account for the increased rate of interest. It is usual for the mortgage also to contain a default clause, the effect of which is to make the principal sum due in its entirety if the mortgagor defaults on the payment of a specified number of instalments.

In many cases where there is a default on the mortgage, the institutional lenders have shown themselves tolerant and understanding, especially in those cases where the problem has arisen from temporary financial difficulties of the mortgagor. They will generally assist the mortgagor to re-arrange his account so that the payments can be maintained at a reduced level, even if this means that payments will have to be made over a longer period. They will not however normally be willing to allow a borrower to suspend payments completely, merely adding the arrears to the capital sum.

If the mortgagor defaults, and the mortgagee wishes to take proceedings, there are two separate claims which he can bring. He can either claim the arrears of instalments, or bring an action for the entire capital sum which has been rendered due by the default clause. If, of course, the mortgagee obtains judgment against the mortgagor, he is entitled, like any judgment creditor, to have the judgment satisfied out of the assets of the mortgagor.

It must however be emphasised that, in such a case, in respect of the mortgagor's property, the mortgagee is in no better position than any other judgment creditor. The mortgagee is in effect suing as if he was an unsecured creditor; the only reason why he will adopt this course is that an action for debt is a relatively simple and straightforward procedure, and recourse to such an action may induce the mortgagor, if his default is due to fecklessness, to mend his ways in the future.

The limitation period for actions on the covenant to repay, since it is a covenant under seal, is twelve years (Limitation Act 1939, s. 2(1), (3)). If the mortgage is not under seal, then the limitation period would be the same as for an ordinary contract debt, that is to say, six years.

In some cases, where the means of the borrower are rather uncertain, it is the practice of mortgagees, before granting the mortgage, to insist on the appointment of a guarantor of the mortgage. In such a case the mortgagee has also the possibility of bringing an action against the guarantor.

It should be noted that this right of action of the personal covenant to repay is additional to the other remedies of the mortgagee. If, for instance, after a sale, the proceeds of sale are insufficient to clear the mortgage debt, the mortgagee can sue the personal covenant to recover the balance remaining due. (*Rudge* v. *Richens* (1873) L.R. 8 C.P. 358).

(b) Entry into possession[1]

Normally, when land is mortgaged, the mortgagor remains in actual possession of the mortgaged property. Under the 1925 legislation, as we have seen, the mortgagor retains the legal fee simple in respect of the mortgaged premises, and the mortgagee takes some lesser interest in the property—either a lease or a charge by way of legal mortgage.

Despite the mortgagor's retention of the fee simple, both Statute (Law of Property Act s. 95(4)) and the courts (*e.g. Alliance Permanent Building Society* v. *Belrum Investments* [1957 I W.L.R. 720; *Four-Maids* v. *Dudley Marshall Properties Ltd.* [1957] Ch. 317) are insistent that, as between mortgagor and mortgagee, it is the mortgagee who has the *right* to possession. This right arises immediately upon the execution of the mortgage; it is in no way dependent upon the legal date for redemption; it is not dependent upon any default by the mortgagor. It is based upon the legal estate or interest which the mortgagee acquires as a result of the mortgage; for this and other purposes, the position of a mortgagee by charge has been assimilated to that of a mortgagee by demise (Law of Property Act s. 87(1) *supra*, p. 13).

Although a mortgagee has, in the absence of a stipulation to the contrary, a right to possession as against the mortgagor, this right is not usually exercised except in the case of a serious default by the mortgagor. In fact, Statute has now intervened in the case of mortgagees of dwellinghouses to restrict the exercise of the right to take possession to those cases where the default of the mortgagor cannot be remedied within a reasonable time (*infra*, p. 57). In addition, there is the purely practical point that Building Societies and other institutional lenders do not *want* possession of the security.

They are primarily interested in securing regular payments of instalments by the mortgagor, and this means that, generally speaking, it is desirable for them to allow the mortgagor to remain in possession of the mortgaged property so as to enable him to earn his living and keep up regular payments of the instalments.

A further factor which inhibits the exercise of the mortgagee's right to possession is the strict liability to account which is placed upon a mortgagee in possession. The liability is a stringent one, and the mortgagee is said to be liable to account to the mortgagor on "a footing of wilful default." This means that a mortgagee in possession has to account to the mortgagor not only for such sums as he actually does receive from the premises, but also for all sums he could possibly have received. Thus, if the mortgagee himself is in possession, he must allow, in computing the interest due to him, for a full rent which could have been received by a notional letting of the property. If he elects to use the powers of leasing which are vested in a mortgagee in possession by section 99 of the Law of Property Act 1925, he must take care to ensure that he obtains the best rent possible from the premises. A neat illustration of the severity of the mortgagee's obligation to account can be seen in the case of *White* v. *City of London Brewery Co.* (1889) 42 Ch. D. 237. In that case the plaintiff mortgaged a public house in the Isle of Dogs to the defendant Brewery. The mortgagor's business failed to prosper, and the defendants exercised their right to take possession of the mortgaged premises. Having taken possession, they granted a lease of the public house to one Moulton; the lease was granted to him subject to a stipulation that he should sell only beer brewed by the defendants. The court held that the defendant brewery was liable to account to the plaintiff not only for the rent which they actually received from letting the public house as a tied house to Moulton, but also for the higher rent which they could have received had they let the house as a free house. The severity of this obligation to account is, in practice, a deterrent of such a kind that mortgagees do not seek possession with a view to letting the mortgaged property; the remedy is usually sought with a view to enabling the mortgagee to exercise his power of sale in such a way that he can give vacant possession to a purchaser.

In addition, many mortgages today contain a clause whereby the mortgagee undertakes not to enforce his right to possession unless there has been a default by the mortgagor. There is even authority to suggest that such a clause may be implied in the normal Building Society mortgage (*Birmingham Citizens Permanent Building Society* v. *Caunt* [1962] Ch. 883, 890). In other cases, a clause is inserted in the mortgage which has the effect of creating a nominal tenancy between the mortgagee and the mortgagor. Such a clause is called an *attornment clause* (*infra*, p. 62) and, if such a clause is present, the mortgagee must take steps to determine the tenancy thus created before the mortgagee can exercise his right to possession (*Hinckley and Country Building Society* v. *Henny* [1953] 1 W.L.R. 352).

Finally, and most importantly, there have been some important changes in the law which substantially restrict the mortgagee's exercise of his right to possession. The history of the matter is somewhat complex, and there have been a number of false starts and hesitations. In addition, there are certain provisions in the Rent Act 1968 which limit the right of a mortgagee to take possession. These will be considered separately.

(i) *General discretion to grant a stay*

Originally, mortgagee's possession actions were dealt with summarily by the common law courts. The courts would grant immediate possession if requested by the mortgagee, and would regard the mortgagee's onerous liability to account whilst in possession as in itself a sufficient deterrent to the unreasonable exercise by him of his right to possession. After the Judicature Acts 1873-75, actions for possessions by mortgagees were heard by the Common Law and Chancery Divisions of the High Court. In 1936, on the recommendation of the Supreme Court Rules Committee, mortgagees' possession actions were transferred to the Chancery Division of the High Court. The Chancery Division, faithful to its old tradition of protecting mortgagors began "to temper the wind to the shorn lamb," and to adjourn the mortgagee's possession action, and thus give the mortgagor an opportunity to pay off the arrears.

In fact, the Chancery Masters (before whom such applications for possession customarily came) began to see their role in such a case as that of "a social worker rather than a judge" (Master Ball, (1961) 77 L.Q.R. 331; Rudden, (1961) Conv. 278). This approach was approved in the case of *Hinckley & South Leicestershire Permanent Benefit Building Society* v. *Freeman* [1941] Ch. 32. But this "tender and vulnerable offshoot from the ancient stem of equity" was not destined to flourish. In *Birmingham Citizens Permanent Building Society* v. *Caunt* [1962] Ch. 883, Russell J., as he then was, excised this shoot as a sucker, and declared that the jurisdiction which had been assumed to grant a stay to the mortgagor was without foundation. The sole power in the court, said Russell J., was to grant an adjournment for a short time (say 28 days) to afford to the mortgagor a chance of paying off the mortgage in full or otherwise remedying his default.

On the recommendation of the Payne Committee (Report of the Committee on the Enforcement of Judgment Debts 1969 (Cmnd. 3909) pp. 355 *et seq.*) Parliament decided to intervene to redress the balance in favour of the mortgagor, despite a suggestion from the Building Societies Association that there was no need for a change (Payne Committee, p. 360). Intervention however, was only to take place in the case of mortgages of dwellinghouses. As we shall see, the original legislation which was enacted to implement the recommendations of the Committee (Administration of Justice Act 1970, ss. 36-38) has proved to be an inadequate answer to the situation, and further amending legislation has had to be introduced. In cases where property other than a dwelling-house is the subject of the mortgage however, none of this legislation applies and the law as stated by Russell J. in *Caunt*'s case must still be taken to govern.

Section 36 of the Act, in effect, gave the court power to adjourn a mortgagee's possession action in respect of land "which consists of or includes a dwellinghouse" if it appeared to the court that in the event of such an adjournment the mortgagor was likely to be able within a reasonable time to pay any sums due under the mortgage or to remedy a default. This power to adjourn was not available to the court in the case of foreclosure proceedings (*infra*, p. 72) as it was thought that in such cases the court already had an inherent jurisdiction to adjourn the case to enable the mortgagor to pay off the debt in full.

The reasons for the change, which were accepted by the Payne Committee (p. 362) lay chiefly in the fact that under present economic conditions it is not unlikely that an increasing number of mortgagors may find themselves temporarily unable to keep up their mortgage instalments, and need the protection of the court against insistent mortgagees, not all of whom are as tolerant as the responsible building societies. In addition, the Payne Committee accepted the principle that an analogous protection to that extended by the Rent Acts to tenants of houses should apply (with some modification) to the mortgagor of a house, in view of the encouragement, by successive governments of the purchase, instead of the renting, of houses by persons of relatively modest means.

Such was the background to the 1970 Act.

This provision, however, proved to be inadequate in those common cases where the mortgage contained a default clause, rendering the whole capital sum due in the event of a default by the mortgagor in respect of one instalment. In *Halifax Building Society* v. *Clark* [1973] Ch. 307, the defendant, Mr. Clark, mortgaged his house to the plaintiff Building Society to secure the sum of £1,530. The original mortgage was made in 1954, but by 1958 Mr. Clark was in arrears with his instalments. Later Mr. Clark deserted his wife, and left her in possession of the mortgaged premises. In 1971, the Building Society commenced possession proceedings against her. The mortgage contained a default clause of the usual type, rendering the capital sum (by now reduced to £1,420) due in the event of a default by the mortgagor in respect of two consecutive monthly instalments.

Now, under section 1(5) of the Matrimonial Homes Act 1967 (discussed further *infra*, p. 61) the mortgagee was obliged to accept payment from the hands of Mrs. Clark, although her husband was apparently the beneficial owner of the house subject to the mortgage. Section 1(5) provides, in effect, that tender or payment made by the wife shall "be as good as if made or done by [the husband]." Relying upon this subsection, Mrs. Clark claimed an adjournment of the mortgagee's action for possession, as she would be in a position, with the help of periodical payments she was receiving from the Department of Social Security, to keep up the instalments in the future, and to pay off the arrears which had accumulated, which then amounted to some £100. This was held by the court to be insufficient to justify the court in exercising its power to adjourn the mortgagee's claim for possession. The sum *due* under the mortgage now amounted to the whole capital sum (namely £1,420) and there was clearly no chance of Mrs. Clark being able to pay off the capital sum within a reasonable period; accordingly there was no question of the court being able to accept that the necessary condition precedent for the grant of relief under section 36 was satisfied. The court then granted an order for possession in twenty-eight days (but *cf.* now *First Middlesborough Trading and Mortgage Co. Ltd.* v. *Cunningham*, *The Times*, February 26, 1974).

The decision seems hard; it might legitimately be supposed that the intention of Parliament, in passing the Act of 1970, had been to improve the lot of mortgagors and their spouses in just such a position as Mrs. Clark (see Baker, [1973] L.Q.R. 117, [1973] Conv. (N.S.) 113, 213). A possible way out of the difficulty would have been to construe "a reasonable period" in section 36(1) of the Act as the whole mortgage term, as has in fact been urged by some writers (see Baker, *loc. cit.*). Parliament, however, decided that it could hardly leave matters until the courts managed to sort things out and that a new attempt must be made. The Administration of Justice Act 1973 contains a section (s. 8) which purports to nullify the decision in *Clark*'s case. Section 8 redefines "sums due under the mortgage" as "such amounts as the mortgagor would have expected to be required to pay if there had been no [default clause]" in other words, the arrears of instalments only. This approach seems to have been adopted in the *First Middlesborough* case (*supra*), decided before the 1973 Act came into force.

It should be noted that the conditions for the grant of an adjournment remain reasonably strict. The court can still only exercise its powers "if it appears to the court that the mortgagor is likely to be able within a reasonable period" to pay the sums due. The burden of proof lies on the mortgagor, to show that the court would be justified in granting a stay. The court shall not exercise its powers (Administration of Justice Act 1973, s. 8(2)) unless it also appears to the court that the mortgagor is likely to be able by the end of the period of adjournment to pay any further amounts that he would have been expected to be required to pay by then. In other words the court should only grant an adjournment if satisfied that the mortgagor can pay off the arrears and keep up his current instalments.

Procedure. Although the mortgagor is entitled to possession, subject to the court's discretion to grant a stay, the mortgagee should not attempt to take possession without a court order. If he attempts to re-enter the premises, he may be guilty of an offence under the Statutes of Forcible Entry, 1381, 1391, and 1429, and (in some cases) under section 31 of the Rent Act 1965, unless, by some chance, the premises had been abandoned by the mortgagor, or the mortgagor consented to the taking of possession. There is normally no need for the mortgagee seeking possession to serve a notice to quit or a demand for possession on the mortgagor. The reason for this seems to be that the interest of the mortgagor in possession of the premises is like that of a tenant at sufferance, who can be ejected without a previous demand for possession (*Thunder d. Weaver* v. *Belcher* (1803) 3 East 449; *Doe d. Roby* v. *Maisey* (1828) 8 B. & C. 767; the suggestion by Lord Mansfield in *Keech* v. *Hall* (1778) 1 Doug. 31 that a mortgagor was a tenant at will is probably erroneous).

To regard a mortgagor as tenant at sufferance of his own home is, to put it mildly, incongruous, and it may be that the law should be amended to require a period of notice to quit to be served on him, as is done with tenants of dwelling-houses under section 16 of the Rent Act 1957.

It has even been held that the notional tenancy created by an attornment clause (*infra*, p. 62) is not caught by section 16 of the Rent Act 1957 so as to require the service of a four week notice to quit on the tenant. In *Alliance Building Society* v. *Pinwill* [1958] Ch. 788, Vaisey J. held that a mortgagor who was a tenant of his mortgagee because of the insertion in the mortgage of an attornment clause was not entitled to the statutory four week notice granted to tenants of dwelling-houses, as the section protected only "a real tenant against a real landlord under a real residential letting." Now, the landlord-tenant relationship created by an attornment clause has been held to have a quite surprising reality in some rather unlikely contexts—for instance, the transmission of the burden of covenants in the "lease" that touch and concern the land within the doctrine of *Spencer*'s case (*infra*, p. 63; and see *Regent Oil Company Ltd.* v. *J. A. Gregory* (*Hatch End*) *Ltd.* [1966] Ch. 402); furthermore, the policy reasons which led Parliament to specify a four week notice period for tenants of residential accommodation (the need to look around for alternative accommodation at a time of housing shortage etc.) would seem to apply, *mutatis mutandis*, to a mortgagor.

Parties to the possession action. Particular difficulties arise in cases where the property is a family dwellinghouse. In such cases, a mortgagor's financial difficulties are often accompanied by matrimonial problems, and the mortgagee may be compelled to resort to proceedings to evict the deserted wife from the former matrimonial home. In those cases, which are now increasingly common, since the Law of Property (Joint Tenants) Act 1964, where the husband and wife both hold the legal title, it is clear that the wife must be made a party to the proceedings. In other cases, where the Matrimonial Homes Act 1967 applies, it is clear that the spouse without a legal interest in the house has a right to compel the mortgagee to accept the payment of instalments by him or her (Matrimonial Homes Act 1967, s. 1(5)).

In *Hastings & Thanet Building Society* v. *Goddard* [1970] 1 W.L.R. 1544, however, the Court of Appeal held that the Matrimonial Homes Act did not give the wife leave to come in as a defendant to possession proceedings in respect of the matrimonial home taken against her mortgagor husband. Worse still, the court went on to observe that there was no statutory justification for the assertion that in any case of a mortgage by a spouse of a matrimonial home the other spouse should be informed if the mortgagor spouse fell into arrears; such a notification would at least enable the other spouse to exercise his or her rights under section 1(5) of the Act. This decision has the disconcerting result that a spouse might find herself, having been deserted, suddenly faced with a demand for possession of the mortgaged premises on the ground of considerable arrears of instalments which, unbeknown to her, had been allowed to accrue by her deserting spouse. It will be particularly difficult for such a spouse, within a reasonable period to accumulate sufficient funds to pay off the arrears and thus justify an adjournment under section 36 of the Administration of Justice Act 1970 (*supra*, p. 57).

In view of the criticism by Megarry J. of the Matrimonial Homes Act in a recent case (*Wroth* v. *Tyler* [1973] 2 W.L.R. 405) it is hoped that reform of this situation will not be long delayed; in the meantime it is difficult to avoid agreeing with the views of a learned commentator, who wrote, *à propos* of the *Goddard* decision "It is proving very difficult to ensure that a spouse—usually a wife—of an owner-occupier ... does not lose her home without fair notice. Joint ownership, where both names are on the legal title, achieves it; other legal techniques are less successful" (F. R. Crane, 1971 Conv. (N.S.) p. 38).

(ii) *Controlled and regulated mortgages*

In these two cases, both of which fall within the Rent Act, there are special statutory restrictions on the right of a mortgagee to take possession. Both types of mortgage are rarely encountered in practice. In the case of a "controlled" mortgage, section 96(1) of the Rent Act 1968 prohibits the mortgagee from taking any steps to "enforce his security" unless the mortgagor is twenty-one days in arrears with his interest or is in breach of some covenant in the mortgage. Entry into possession has been held to be an attempt "to enforce his security" (*Martin* v. *Watson & Egan* [1919] 2 I.R. 332). In the case of a regulated mortgage, which falls within section 94(1) of the Rent Act 1968, the mortgagee's right to possess is subject to the court's power to grant relief to the mortgagor if the mortgagor would suffer "severe financial hardship" because of (a) the step taken by the mortgagee to enforce his security and (b) the operation of the Rent Act. Further details of the operation of these complex provisions are to be found elsewhere (see *e.g.* Megarry, *The Rent Acts*, 10th ed., Vol. I, pp. 479-497).

(iii) *Attornment clauses*

These are sometimes of particular importance in cases where a mortgagee is taking possession proceedings. The effect of such a clause is to make the mortgagor a tenant (usually at a nominal rent) of the mortgagee. The purpose of such a clause was, in former times, to enable the mortgagee to take advantage of a special procedure to evict tenants laid down by the Small Tenements Recovery Act 1838, and also (possibly) to distrain for mortgage interest, if the rent reserved under the attornment clause was the same as the interest due under the mortgage. These supposed advantages have now disappeared (Bills of Sale Acts 1878 and 1882, and Rent Act 1965) and it may be wondered why such clauses continue to appear in mortgages today. The answer probably lies in inertia and conservatism; but a mortgagee seeking possession must first take care to determine by due notice any tenancy created by an attornment clause (*supra*, p. 55), unless the tenancy is made self-determining in the event of a default by the mortgagor. Such clauses may however have received a new lease of life as a result of the decision in *Regent Oil Co.* v. *J. A. Gregory (Hatch End) Ltd.* [1966] Ch. 402. It was held in that case that a covenant in the mortgage tying the mortgagor to sell only the petroleum products of the mortgagee was a covenant which touched and concerned the land of the mortgagor (who was also a tenant of the mortgagee by virtue of an attornment clause) and thus bound a purchaser of the equity of redemption. In general, attornment clauses are nowadays regarded as redundant, and most authorities advise their omission (*e.g.* Wurtzburg & Mills, *Building Society Law*, pp. 198-199; Fisher & Lightwood, *Mortgages*, p. 32).

(iv) *Limitation*

If a mortgagee retains possession for twelve years without acknowledging the mortgagor's title, or receiving any payment of principal and interest from him, the right to redeem is extinguished under section 12 of the Limitation Act 1939, although the period may be extended in certain cases. This rule is of comparatively little importance, since the purpose of most mortgagees in obtaining possession is to enable a speedy sale with vacant possession to take place.

(c) Power of sale[2]

In practice, this is the remedy of the mortgagee which is most commonly used, in conjunction with entry into possession. The great advantage, from the mortgagee's point of view, of the power of sale, is that it enables the mortgagee to recover his capital without difficulty so that he can invest it elsewhere. Before exercising his power of sale, the mortgagee will normally seek vacant possession of the mortgaged property so as to enable him to secure a good price on the sale (see *infra*, p. 68).

Existence of the power

At common law, a mortgagee had no effective power of sale; he could of course, transfer his mortgage, but the mortgagee would take the property subject to the equity of redemption vested in the mortgagor. The only way in which this difficulty could be evaded would be for the mortgagee to seek to foreclose first; the foreclosure, if successful, would extinguish the equity of redemption (see *infra*, p. 72) and then the mortgagee could transfer an unencumbered fee simple to the purchaser. This, however, was an inconvenient and cumbersome process, and so the practice grew up of inserting in the mortgage itself a clause giving the mortgagee an express power of sale over the mortgaged property. The Conveyancing Act of 1881, implied such a power of sale in most legal mortgages, and the provisions of that Act have now been repeated and extended somewhat in the Laws of Property Act 1925.

The Act provides (s. 101) that the mortgagee's power of sale shall arise if three conditions are fulfilled:

(i) the mortgage must be by deed (s. 101(1)(*c*))

(ii) the mortgage money must be due—in other words, the legal date for redemption must have passed (*supra*, p. 8). Commonly an express clause fixing the legal date for redemption is inserted; but if there is no such clause and the mortgage is an instalment mortgage, the power arises and the money is regarded as due as soon as any instalment is due and unpaid (*Payne* v. *Cardiff R.D.C.* [1932] 1 K.B. 241).

(iii) there is no contrary intention in the mortgage deed (s. 101(4)).

If these conditions are fulfilled, the power of sale *arises*; but the Act further goes on to provide that the power of sale shall only be *exercisable* if one of certain other conditions is fulfilled, that is to say, either:

(a) Notice requiring repayment of the mortgage money has been served on the mortgagor or one of two or more mortgagors, and default has been made in payment of the mortgage money, or of part thereof, for three months after such service: or

(b) Some interest under the mortgage is in arrears and unpaid for two months after becoming due: or

(c) There has been a breach of some provision contained in the mortgage deed or in the Law of Property Act on the part of the mortgagor, the provision not being a provision for payment of the mortgage money or interest thereon (s. 103).

The importance of this distinction between the power arising and the power being exercisable is considerable. Unless the power has *arisen*, the mortgagee has no power of sale at all; any purported sale by him will not be effective to transfer the legal estate to a purchaser, but will vest in the purchaser only the rights of mortgagee as *mortgagee*, and so will only operate as a transfer of mortgage. Clearly, therefore, a purchaser must ascertain that the power of sale has *arisen*. The question of *exercisability*, however, is not a question which normally concerns a purchaser, as this is a matter between the mortgagor and the mortgagee.

If the power has not arisen, we have seen that the purchaser from the mortgagee does not get a good title. For this reason, a conveyance on sale by a mortgagee in purported exercise of his statutory power is not a good root of title, and title should commence from the document creating the power, and not the document which purports to be an exercise of the power (see Farrand, *Contract and Conveyance*, p. 97).

If the power has arisen and is exercisable, it is clear that a purchaser gets a good title and the mortgagor has no recourse against the selling mortgagee, unless he can show that the power was *improperly exercised* (*i.e.* that there has been some impropriety in the *manner* of the exercise of the power).

If the power has arisen, but is not exercisable, then, prima facie, the purchaser gets a good title, but the mortgagor has a remedy in damages against the selling mortgagee (Law of Property Act s. 104(2)). To this, however, an exception seems to exist. It has been held that in a case where the purchaser is *aware* that the power is not exercisable, his title will be impeachable at the suit of the mortgagor. The cases which establish this apparent exception, however, are, for the most part, based upon express (as opposed to statutory) powers of sale, and generally precede the 1925 legislation. In *Selwyn* v. *Garfit* (1888) 38 Ch. D. 273, for instance, the court decided that the title of the purchaser from the mortgagee was bad, but the case was entirely concerned with an express power of sale. In *Bailey* v. *Barnes* [1894] 1 Ch. 25 there are some suggestions that a similar result would follow in the case of the statutory power given to mortgagees under the Conveyancing Act 1881, and these dicta have been approved *obiter* in the post 1925 case of *Lord Waring* v. *London and Manchester Assurance Co. Ltd.* [1935] Ch. 310. It may be noted, however, that in none of these cases has the court had to consider expressly the wording of section 104 of the Law of Property Act, which provides (in subsection (2)) that "the title of the purchaser shall not be impeachable on the ground ... that the power was ... improperly or irregularly exercised." There are dicta that "to uphold the title of a purchaser who had notice of impropriety or irregularity in the exercise of the power of sale would be to convert the provisions of the Statute into an instrument of fraud" (*Bailey* v. *Barnes*, *supra*, at p. 30), but it is not altogether clear whether these dicta will prevail against the clear wording of the Statute.

If these dicta are correct, it seems that notice in the context of a purchaser from a mortgagee bears a meaning rather different from that which usually applies. It seems that there is no obligation upon a purchaser from a mortgagee to make the enquiries which a suspicious purchaser should make, and that a purchaser will *not* have constructive notice of any impropriety in the exercise of the power of sale which would have been revealed by such enquiries (*Bailey* v. *Barnes*, *supra*, at p. 34). If this anomalous rule is still to exist, there seems to be no good reason in principle why a purchaser from a mortgagee should be treated with greater solicitude than is normally shown to purchasers.

It should be noted that the power of sale is exercisable by any mortgagee. In the case of a sale by the first mortgagee, there is no problem as he will usually have the title deeds and can vest an unencumbered fee simple in the purchaser. A second or subsequent mortgagee can usually only sell *subject* to prior encumbrances, unless the prior mortgagee concurs in the sale, in which case the prior mortgagee will have first claim on the proceeds of sale (Law of Property Act ss. 89, 105). There is, however, a complication in cases where the title to the land is registered under the Land Registration Act 1925. In that case a prospective purchaser from a mortgagee who is selling under his statutory power can insist upon the selling mortgagee procuring his registrations as proprietor of the charge (Land Registration Act s. 110(5)). This cannot be done unless the first mortgagee (with whom the land certificate may have been deposited *supra*, p. 21) will co-operate by lodging the land certificate with the Registry. As an alternative, the purchaser can require the mortgagee to procure a disposition from the proprietor to the purchaser, but this is a dangerous procedure as such a disposition will not be an exercise of the mortgagee's power of sale within section 34 of the Act, and will not overreach subsequent charges (*Re White Rose Cottage* [1965] Ch. 940, Hayton, *Registered Land*, p. 125).

The effect of a sale by a mortgagee is to vest the legal estate (which until the sale had been in the mortgagor) in the purchaser (Law of Property Act s. 88). In the case of registered land, of course, the purchaser's title is only completed when he procures his own substantive registration as proprietor (Land Registration Act s. 19). The purchaser will take the land subject to mortgages which have priority to the mortgage of the selling mortgagee, unless the prior mortgagee concurs in the sale. Subsequent mortgages, and the equity of redemption of the mortgagor, will not concern the purchaser as they will be overreached and take effect in the proceeds of sale (Law of Property Act s. 2(1)(iii)).

A sale by a mortgagee clearly precludes redemption by the mortgagor, since his equity of redemption becomes a right against the proceeds of sale. Even a contract for the sale of the mortgaged property will preclude redemption, as the contract is effective in equity to transfer the fee simple to the purchaser, under the equitable doctrine of conversion. It is in effect the contract which amounts in substance to the exercise by the mortgagee of his powers (see *Waring* v. *London and Manchester Assurance Co.* (*supra*, p. 61); *Property & Bloodstock Ltd.* v. *Emerton* [1968] Ch. 94; *Duke* v. *Robson* [1973] 1 W.L.R. 267).

Price

A particular problem concerns the price to be obtained by a mortgagee when selling in the exercise of his power. The question is clearly of some importance to the mortgagor, as the balance (after satisfaction of the mortgage debts of the selling mortgagee and other mortgagees) should be paid to him under section 105 of the Law of Property Act (*infra*, p. 31). A mortgagee might be tempted to sell for a sum just sufficient to cover the mortgage debt, and thus leave the mortgagor without the surplus he was expecting from the sale. It used to be thought that so long as the sale was made in good faith, the mortgagor could not complain. In the case of Building Societies, Parliament intervened, and the Building Societies Act 1962 (replacing earlier legislation) imposes a duty (s. 36) upon a Building Society to take reasonable care to ensure that the price for which the property is sold is the best price that can reasonably be obtained. This rule was thought to place a more onerous duty upon a Building Society mortgagee than upon other mortgagees (*Reliance Permanent Building Society* v. *Harwood-Stamper* [1944] Ch. 362).

It now seems however, that a Building Society may be in

no different position from any other mortgagee, and that the rule contained in the Building Societies Act is purely declaratory of the rule imposed by the common law. In *Cuckmere Brick Co. Ltd.* v. *Mutual Finance Ltd.* [1971] Ch. 948 the Court of Appeal held that a mortgagee is under a duty "to take reasonable care to obtain the true market value of the mortgaged property" (*per* Salmon L.J. at p. 966). On the facts of that case, a majority of the Court of Appeal held that the mortgagee had not done so, and was thus liable in damages to the mortgagor. In that case, a mortgagee was exercising his power of sale in respect of a plot of building land at Maidstone. The plot was advertised by the selling agents as having planning permission for the erection of thirty-three detached houses. In the event, such planning permission did exist, but there was also in being planning permission for the erection of 100 flats, which the mortgagor had also contemplated building at one stage. The flat permission was not mentioned in the advertisement of the auction of the mortgaged plot. At auction, the plot fetched £44,000, which was actually insufficient to cover the mortgage debt of £50,000. Thus the mortgagee was already out of pocket when the mortgagor commenced proceedings against him, arguing that had the advertisement made clear that planning permission for flats was also in existence, a higher price could have been obtained.

The court accepted the mortgagor's contention, and held that a higher price—probably in the region of £65,000—could have been obtained, if the plot had been advertised as having permission for the erection of flats. It was thus held that the mortgagee was in breach of his duty to the mortgagor, and that he was liable in damages to him. The burden of proof, however, is on the mortgagor, and is a heavy one. The mere fact that a mortgagee sells without mentioning *e.g.* a planning permission, of which he is ignorant does not, without more, justify a finding of negligence on the part of the mortgagee (*Palmer* v. *Barclays Bank* (1972) 23 P. & C.R. 30).

A number of questions remain. First, does a mortgagee

discharge his duty to the mortgagor if he places the sale in the hands of a reputable agent, as actually was the case in *Cuckmere*? The point was not actually decided in the case, since it did not arise on the pleadings, but is obviously of considerable practical importance. Cross L.J., *obiter*, was of opinion that the mortgagee might still be liable for the negligence of his independent contractor, and then went on to suggest that the mortgagor might himself have an action against the agent for negligence. This last suggestion seems a curious one; normally, if A gives negligent advice to B causing purely economic loss to C, a third party, there is no duty owed by A to C (see *Winfield & Jolowicz on Tort*, pp. 242-243). It does not seem unreasonable that a mortgagee should be held liable for the negligence of his agent, since the mortgagor has no say in the selection of the agent and the mortgagee does. In the same way, recent authority is broadly in favour of making a vendor liable for the loss of a pre-contract deposit paid to an agent selected by him (see *Burt* v. *Claude Cousins* [1971] 2 Q.B. 426; *Barrington* v. *Lee* [1972] 1 Q.B. 326 is to the contrary).

Secondly, what is the position of a purchaser? The purchaser was not a party to the proceedings in the *Cuckmere* case, and one assumes that in most cases he can rely on the protection afforded by section 104(2) of the Law of Property Act. As we have seen, however, this section possibly affords no protection to a purchaser who knows of an irregularity in the exercise of the power of sale. Suppose for instance that the purchaser of the building plot in the *Cuckmere* case had known of the existence of the flat planning permission, and had bought the plot at a bargain price? It might conceivably be held by analogy with *Selwyn* v. *Garfit* (*supra*, p. 66) that his title was impeachable and that he had taken only a transfer of the mortgage and took subject to the equity of redemption still vested in the mortgagor. There is no *statutory* presumption in favour of a purchaser from a mortgagee, as there is in the case of a purchaser of settled land from a tenant for life (Settled Land Act 1925, s. 110(1)) that he has given the best price.

Thirdly, how strict is the mortgagee's duty? Some sort of negligence is needed to render him liable. He is not bound (for instance) to sell by auction (*Davey* v. *Durrant* (1857) 1 De. G. & J. 535, 560), nor is he bound to wait for a propitious movement in the market. As Salmon L.J. put it in the *Cuckmere* case "He has the right to realise his security by turning it into money when he likes." Is the mortgagee obliged to indulge in the morally objectionable but legally unexceptionable practice of "gazumping"?—*i.e.* accepting a higher offer after a previous (subject to contract) offer has been accepted? It has been held that a trustee for sale is under a fiduciary duty *vis à vis* his beneficiaries, to gazump (*Buttle* v. *Saunders* [1950] W.N. 255). Is a mortgagee under a similar duty?

Finally, the relationship between the *Cuckmere* decision and the special statutory duty placed on Building Societies under section 36 of the Building Societies Act (*supra*, p. 68) is obscure. It was always thought that the Building Societies had been singled out for special attention by Parliament. Is the Act after all declaratory of the common law? Or is there some mysterious difference between a "proper market price" (*Cuckmere*) and "the best price reasonably obtainable" (Building Societies Act—applied in *Harwood-Stamper*'s case, *supra*). Salmon L.J., in *Cuckmere*, could see no real difference between them (p. 966).

Proceeds of sale

Although it has often been said that a mortgagee is not a trustee of his power of sale (see *Cuckmere Brick*, *supra*) he *is* a trustee of the proceeds of sale, by statute. Section 105 of the Law of Property Act 1925, provides that the proceeds of sale shall be held by the mortgagee "in trust to be applied by him, first, in payment of all costs, charges and expenses properly incurred by him as incident to the sale, or any attempted sale, or otherwise; secondly, in discharge of the mortgage money, interest, and costs, and other money, if any, due under the mortgage; and the residue of the money received shall be paid to the person entitled to the mortgaged property...." The concluding words of this section are odd; the person, strictly speaking, entitled to the mortgaged property after the sale is the purchaser (except that the property is no longer mortgaged). The Act is generally taken to mean that the surplus should be paid to a subsequent mortgagee (if any), or, if there is none, to the mortgagor, as the person *formerly* entitled to the mortgaged property.

To be on the safe side, a mortgagee who has exercised his power of sale should search the Land Charges Registry (or in the case of Registered Land, the Land Registry) to see if there are any mortgages which have been registered subsequently to his own. If none have been registered, but the mortgagee has actual or constructive notice of a later mortgagee, he should probably still pay the surplus to that mortgagee, for otherwise he will be in breach of trust. It is thought that the usual sanction for non-registration (that the incumbrance shall be "void against a purchaser") (Land Charges Act 1972, s. 4(6)) is irrelevant, as there is no question of enforceability against a purchaser arising here.

(d) Foreclosure[3]

This is the most drastic of the remedies available to the mortgagee. It amounts to a total abolition of the mortgagor's equity of redemption, so that the mortgagee becomes entitled to the property freed and discharged from the equity of redemption. Before 1925, the legal estate was already vested in the mortgagee by virtue of the mortgage; after 1925, as we have seen, the legal estate remains vested in the mortgagor (*supra*, p. 11). The effect in law of a successful foreclosure is now different since the effect of a foreclosure decree absolute (a term which will be explained later) is to transfer the legal estate from the mortgagor to the mortgagee (Law of Property Act 1925, ss. 88(2), 89(2)). In the case of registered land, an order for foreclosure is completed by the registration of the proprietor of the charge as the proprietor of the land, and by the cancellation of the charge (Land Registration Act 1925, s. 34(3)).

Because of its drastic nature, the right of a mortgagee to foreclose is hedged around with a number of stringent procedural safeguards, and, nowadays, it is not a remedy which is commonly sought by mortgagees, since it is generally quicker and more expeditious to exercise the power of sale, after an entry into possession. The fact that the court could not grant a stay of the mortgagee's possession claim in an action for foreclosure has now been remedied by Statute (Administration of Justice Act 1973, s. 8(3)). Foreclosure can only take place by court order, and the courts have shown a very proper reluctance to grant foreclosure decrees. Their reluctance is likely to be all the greater at a time of increasing property values, since the effect of a foreclosure may, in such circumstances, amount to allowing the mortgagee to acquire the mortgaged property at a considerable undervalue.

The right to foreclose does not arise at all until the legal date of redemption has passed (*supra*, p. 8). We have seen that the essence of a foreclosure decree is that a court of equity is destroying that which the court itself created, namely, the equity of redemption. Clearly, foreclosure proceedings are inappropriate until the equitable right to redeem has itself arisen.

Foreclosure proceedings have an important impact on all persons who claim an interest in the equity of redemption. These persons include, besides the mortgagor, any mortgagees who rank in priority below the foreclosing mortgagee. Such mortgagees are only mortgagees of the equity of redemption, and, clearly, if the equity of redemption is abolished, it follows that the security of such mortgagees will be abolished too. Hence, it is a rule in foreclosure proceedings that the mortgagor and any mortgagees ranking in priority below the foreclosing mortgagee must be made parties to the foreclosure proceedings. This gives them a chance to preserve their security by redeeming (*i.e.* paying off) the mortgage of the foreclosing mortgagee, or to apply for a judicial sale. We have seen that in the case of a sale by a mortgagee, there is a strict order regulating the priority of payment of mortgagees, so that each mortgagee in turn receives what is due to him (and no more); the court will normally defer to the claims of subsequent mortgagees threatened with loss of their security by foreclosure proceedings commenced by a prior mortgagee to the extent of ordering a sale if one is requested, since the prior mortgagee will have first helping from the proceeds of sale (Law of Property Act s. 105, *supra*, p. 71).

A foreclosure decree is granted in stages. At the hearing of the mortgagee's action for foreclosure, the court may grant a foreclosure order *nisi*, *i.e.* an order that an account be taken to determine the amount due to the mortgagee under the mortgage, and a direction that if this sum is not paid within six months (thus giving the mortgagor yet another chance to redeem) the foreclosure shall become absolute. Even the grant of a foreclosure order absolute to the mortgagee is not necessarily the end of the day. The court will in some circumstances re-open even a foreclosure order absolute, so as to allow the mortgagor to redeem, even though the general effect of a foreclosure order absolute is to extinguish for ever the mortgagor's right to redeem. The court has a general discretion in the matter, which is usually exercised leniently in favour of mortgagors, but the relevant principles were discussed by Sir G. Jessel M.R. in the leading case of *Campbell* v. *Holyland* (1877) 7 Ch. D. 166. He said:

> "An order for foreclosure, according to the practice of the old Court of Chancery, was never really absolute, nor can it be so now ... [The mortgagor seeking to re-open] must come, as it is said promptly; that is within a reasonable time.... Was the mortgagor entitled to redeem, but by some accident unable to redeem? Did he expect to get the money from a quarter from which he might reasonably hope to obtain it, and was he disappointed at the last moment? Then an element for consideration has always been the nature of the property as regards value. For instance, if an estate were worth £50,000, and had been foreclosed for a mortgage debt of £5,000, the man who came to redeem that estate would have a longer time than when the estate was worth £5,100, and he was foreclosed

for £5,000. But not only is there money value; there may be other considerations. It may be an old family estate, or a chattel, or picture, which possesses a special value for the mortgagor, but which possesses not the same value for other people....

Then it is said you must not interfere against purchasers ... there are purchasers and purchasers. If the purchaser buys ... after the lapse of a considerable time from the order of foreclosure absolute, with no notice of any extraneous circumstances which would induce the Court to interfere, I for one should decline to interfere with such a title as that; but if the purchaser bought the estate within twenty-four hours after the foreclosure absolute, and with notice of the fact that it was of much greater value than the amount of the mortgage debt, is it to be supposed that a Court of Equity would listen to the contention of such a purchaser that he ought not to be interfered with? ..."

In all the circumstances, it may be doubted whether the remedy of foreclosure has much part to play in the modern law of mortgages. Courts are likely to be reluctant to grant foreclosure decrees in a time of increasing property values, when a 90 per cent. mortgage may become, in a relatively short period, a 50 per cent. mortgage. Purchasers from mortgagees who have foreclosed run the risk of having the foreclosure re-opened. The power of sale is more useful, more convenient, and safer for purchasers: might it not be worth following the example of the Republic of Ireland and replacing foreclosure by an order for a judicial sale? The power to order sale in foreclosure proceedings already exists (Law of Property Act s. 91(2)); all that is suggested is that this section might be expanded to replace foreclosure.

(e) Appointment of a receiver[4]

This is a remedy which is useful when the mortgagee fears that his interest payments are in jeopardy, but does not wish to exercise his power of sale so as to recover his capital to enable him to re-invest elsewhere. He has a power, in certain circumstances, to appoint a receiver who will collect the rents and profits of the premises, and use them, in part at least to defray the interest payments due under the mortgage. The power is not, of course, of much practical use to a mortgagee in the ordinary case of a mortgage of an owner-occupied dwellinghouse, since there will then be nothing for a receiver to receive, and a mortgagee will usually find it more advantageous to go into possession and sell the premises, if an action for debt in respect of arrears of interest on the mortgage has been unsuccessful. The power to appoint a receiver may be useful in some cases still, however, as when the mortgaged property is a block of flats, and the receiver can collect the rent from the tenants and hand it over to the mortgagee.

In former times, it was customary for the mortgage to contain an express clause authorising the appointment of a receiver. Such express clauses are now rare, as there is a statutory power to appoint a receiver (Law of Property Act s. 101(1)(ii). The power to appoint a receiver *arises* and is exercisable in the same circumstances and under the same conditions as the statutory power of sale. In those cases where the title to the land is registered, the power to appoint a receiver is subject to the same tiresome difficulty that we noticed above in connection with the power of sale, namely that the mortgagee can only exercise his power after he has procured his own substantive registration as the proprietor of the charge (see *supra*, p. 67 and *Lever Finance Ltd.* v. *Needleman's Trustee* [1956] Ch. 375). Just as a purchaser is not concerned to see that the power of sale is properly exercised a person paying rent etc. to a receiver is not concerned to see that the power to appoint a receiver was exercisable (Law of Property Act s. 109(4)).

The receiver must be appointed in writing (s. 109(1)) and may be removed or replaced in like manner (s. 109(5)). Though appointed and selected by the mortgagee, he is deemed to be the agent of the mortgagor, who, in the absence of a contrary provision in the mortgage, remains liable for his acts and defaults (s. 109(2)). A mortgagor thus remains liable on his personal covenant to pay interest if a receiver has been appointed by the mortgagee who then absconds with the rents (*White* v. *Metcalf* [1903] 2 Ch. 567. The mortgagor could not, of course, recover further rents from the tenants, as the receipt of the receiver would be a good discharge for the tenants (s. 109(3)).

It is provided by Statute that the receiver shall apply all moneys received by him in the following order: (s. 109(8)).

(i) In discharge of all rents, taxes, rates and outgoings whatever affecting the mortgaged property; and

(ii) in keeping down all annual sums or other payments, and the interest on all principal sums, having priority to the mortgage in right whereof he is receiver; and

(iii) in payment of his commission, and of the premiums on fire, life, or other insurances, if any, properly payable under the mortgage deed or under the Act, and the cost of executing necessary or proper repairs directed in writing by the mortgagee; and

(iv) in payment of the interest accruing due in respect of any principal money due under the mortgage; and

(v) in or towards discharge of the principal money if so directed in writing by the mortgagee; and shall pay the residue if any of the money received by him to the person who, but for the possession of the receiver, would have been entitled to receive the income of which he is appointed receiver, or who is otherwise entitled to the mortgaged property.

(f) Custody of title deeds

This is not, strictly speaking, a *remedy* of a mortgagee, but it is an important part of his rights as mortgagee, since the possession of the title deeds by the mortgagee will usually make it difficult for the mortgagor to raise further loans on the security of the property or otherwise deal with it to the disadvantage of the mortgagee. The absence of title deeds will usually constitute notice to a subsequent mortgagee that the property is subject to a mortgage. Before 1926, a mortgagee was entitled to possession of the title deeds of the mortgaged property as an incident of his entitlement to the legal estate (*supra*, p. 5); now section 85(1) of the Law of Property Act 1925 gives a similar right to a mortgagee by demise or charge. A mortgagee who has not got possession of the title deeds (*e.g.* because they are in the hands of a prior mortgagee) may call upon the mortgagee holding the title deeds to produce them to him so that he can, if he wishes to exercise his power of sale, prove his title to a purchaser who is to take the property subject to the prior mortgage.

As we shall see later, the possession (or non-possession) of the title deeds by a mortgagee may have an important effect upon questions of priority between mortgagees.

In the case of registered land, there are of course no title deeds of which the mortgagee can take possession. Accordingly, a different procedure obtains. In the case of a registered charge (the most common case) (*supra*, p. 16) the mortgagor deposits his land certificate with the Land Registry, who then issue a "Charge Certificate" to the mortgagee as proprietor of the registered charge (Land Registration Act 1925, s. 27). There is also the possibility of a mortgage by a deposit of the Land Certificate, and this procedure is commonly adopted for short term loans. This practice, however, is not without its difficulties (see p. 21) especially as regards priorities.

Rights and Remedies of Equitable Mortgagees

In the case of equitable mortgagees, rather different principles apply. An equitable mortgagee, by definition, takes no legal estate in the land; also, some of the provisions of the Law of Property Act are not applicable in his case. The mortgage will normally contain an express covenant for repayment, like a legal mortgage, and the mortgagee can, like a legal mortgagee, take proceedings for debt in respect of any arrears.

The position with regard to the right of an equitable

mortgagee to take possession of the mortgaged property is far from clear. To avoid these difficulties, many equitable mortgages contain a clause empowering the mortgagee to take possession of the property in the event of a default by the mortgagor. In such cases, the provisions of the Administration of Justice Acts 1970 and 1973, apply to possession claims by an equitable mortgagee (*supra*, p. 56). Another device which is sometimes used is the insertion into the equitable mortgage of a clause granting a power of attorney to the mortgagee to enable him to "convert" his equitable mortgage into a legal mortgage by the execution of a legal mortgage; this makes available to the mortgagee all the rights and remedies of a legal mortgagee, including the right to take possession of the mortgaged property (see *McCarthy & Stone Ltd.* v. *Hodge Ltd.* [1971] 1 W.L.R. 1547.

In the absence of some such device, it is doubtful whether an equitable mortgagee can claim the right to go into possession of the mortgaged property. We have seen that in the case of a legal mortgagee, his right used to be based upon his possession of the legal estate, and is now based upon his possession of a term of years or its equivalent (s. 87(1)) in the case of a mortgagee by charge. *Ex hypothesi*, an equitable mortgagee has no legal estate on which his claim to possession can be based. It has been urged (see Megarry & Wade, *The Law of Real Property*, 3rd ed., p. 917) that an equitable mortgagee has a right to take possession under the doctrine of *Walsh* v. *Lonsdale* ((1882) 21 Ch. D. 9—and see also 70 L.Q.R. 161, 71 L.Q.R. 204, where the authorities are fully reviewed). This suggestion is not universally accepted (see *e.g.* Cheshire, *Modern Law of Real Property*, p. 669) and it may be that an equitable mortgage is an interest in property which is independent from the doctrine of *Walsh* v. *Lonsdale*; indeed, if an equitable mortgage is an equitable interest in property of the *Walsh* v. *Lonsdale* type, some very inconvenient consequences may follow in respect of priority of such interests (*infra*, p. 103).

If an equitable mortgage is not made by deed, the mortgagee cannot claim the statutory power of sale implied in mortgages by section 101(1) of the Law of Property Act since that power only arises if the mortgage is made by deed. To evade this difficulty, it is customary for equitable mortgages today to be made by deed, since a mortgagee will usually find that the power of sale is his most efficacious remedy in practice. Even if the mortgage is made by deed, a further difficulty arises from the decision in *Re Hodson & Howes Contract* (1887) 35 Ch. D. 668. That case concerned the statutory power of sale conferred on a mortgagee under the Conveyancing Act 1881, which was in similar terms to that now contained in the Law of Property Act 1925. Hodson, an equitable mortgagee, took out a Vendor and Purchaser summons to determine whether he, as an equitable mortgagee, could convey the legal estate in the mortgaged property to a purchaser. The power is a power "to sell the mortgaged property" and it was held in the case that the expression "the mortgaged property" was confined to the property the mortgagee had, namely an equitable interest. As North J. put it: "He can convey all he has; but he cannot convey the legal estate." This decision was subsequently confirmed by the Court of Appeal. Later dicta in *Re White Rose Cottage* [1965] Ch. 940, 951, from the same court suggest that section 104(1) of the Law of Property Act 1925 gives an equitable mortgagee power to sell the legal estate, but the status of these dicta is far from clear, although they are approved by Fisher & Lightwood, *Mortgages*, p. 318. To avoid all these difficulties, it is usual for an equitable mortgage to contain some device which will enable the mortgagee to convey the legal estate. These devices take two common forms:

(a) *Power of attorney*. A power of attorney might be granted to the mortgagee empowering the mortgagee to convey the legal estate which remains vested, until sale, in the mortgagor. Such a power is irrevocable, under section 4(1) of the Powers of Attorney Act 1971, as it is given to secure a proprietary interest of the donee of the power; thus, both the mortgagee and a purchaser from him who buys in reliance on the power are protected (section 5(3) of the Powers of Attorney Act 1971). A purchaser is "entitled to assume that the power is incapable of revocation, "and a purchaser should not enquire beyond the face of such a power.

(b) *Declaration of trust*. A clause is inserted in the mortgage whereby the mortgagor declares that he holds the legal estate on trust for the mortgagee, and authorises the mortgagee to appoint himself or his nominee as trustee in place of the mortgagor, to enable a conveyance of the legal estate to a purchaser to take place.

A sale by an equitable mortgagee is, of course, subject to the same restrictions, as to price etc., as a sale by a legal mortgagee (*Palmer* v. *Barclays Bank*, *supra*, p. 69).

Appointment of a receiver

Again, the general rule is that the power to appoint a receiver arises only if the mortgage is made by deed. For this reason, it is usual to make an equitable mortgage under seal. Then section 109 applies as it does to a legal mortgage, and there is a statutory power to appoint a receiver. In the absence of a statutory power (for instance if the mortgage is not made by deed) the High Court has power on application by the mortgagee to appoint a receiver "in all cases in which it appears to the court to be just or convenient to do so" (section 45(4) of the Supreme Court of Justice Act 1925). A court will normally do so if, for instance, interest due under the mortgage is in arrear.

Foreclosure

In the case of an equitable mortgage, the court has jurisdiction to foreclose, or to order a judicial sale in lieu of foreclosure. The foreclosure order takes a rather different form from that usual in the case of a legal mortgage, as it consists of an order to the defendant mortgagor to convey the legal title to the foreclosing mortgagee.

Notes

[1] See also, Megarry and Wade, p. 908; Cheshire, p. 660; Waldock, p. 233; Fisher and Lightwood, pp. 269-303; Nokes, p. 61.

[2] See also, Megarry and Wade, p. 902; Cheshire, p. 653; Waldock, pp. 248-260, 367-381; Nokes, pp. 52-57; Fisher and Lightwood, pp. 303-327.

[3] See also, Megarry and Wade, p. 899; Cheshire, p. 657; Waldock, p. 352; Nokes, p. 65; Fisher and Lightwood, p. 329.

[4] See also, Megarry and Wade, p. 912; Cheshire, p. 661; Nokes, p. 57; Waldock, p. 241; Fisher and Lightwood, p. 256.

CHAPTER 6

OTHER MATTERS INCIDENT TO THE MORTGAGE RELATIONSHIP

1. POWERS OF LEASING[1]

WE have seen (*supra*, p. 40) that any leases validly granted by the mortgagor before the mortgage will be binding on the mortgagee. At common law, the rule was that during the currency of the mortgage, neither mortgagor nor mortgagee could create a lease binding on the other party without his consent; the lease would of course bind the grantor of the lease as a matter of contract. There are a few exceptions to this principle—for instance, if the mortgagee "adopts" a lease granted by the mortgagor—and these will still be of some importance where the statutory power of granting leases is for some reason inapplicable. The common law principle of inability to grant leases has been to some extent abrogated by Statute. Section 99 of the Law of Property Act 1925 gives a statutory power of leasing, but this power can be excluded by a contrary provision in the mortgage deed (Law of Property Act 1925, s. 99(13)). In practice, as we shall see, it is commonly excluded in Building Society mortgages and mortgages granted by other institutional lenders, as they are anxious to preserve the value of their security, which could be imperilled if the mortgagor were to grant a tenancy which was protected by the Rent Act and which was binding on the mortgagee.

The statutory power

This is contained in section 99 of the Law of Property Act 1925. Generally, it gives a power to both mortgagor and mortgagee to create leases binding upon each other, subject to fairly stringent conditions to protect the security. These conditions are roughly analogous to those imposed on a tenant for life under section 42 of the Settled Land Act, and are designed for a similar purpose, namely to ensure that the long term management of the land is not imperilled by the exercise of the leasing power. The conditions are as follows:

(a) *Possession*

The power can only be exercised by a mortgagor in possession, a mortgagee in possession, or by a mortgagee who has appointed a receiver who is still acting (Law of Property Act s. 99(1), (2), (19)).

(b) *Duration*

The lease must not exceed fifty years for an agricultural or occupation lease, or 999 years for a building lease (s. 99(3)).

(c) *Taking effect in possession*

The lease must be limited to take effect in possession not more than twelve months after its date (s. 99(5)).

(d) *Rent*

The lease must in general be at a full rent (s. 99(9)), and contain a covenant for payment of rent by the lessee and a right of re-entry for non-payment of rent (s. 99(7)).

(e) *Counterpart lease*

A counterpart lease must be executed by the lessee and delivered to the lessor (s. 99(8)).

Exclusion of the statutory power

In general, the statutory power of leasing is commonly excluded, as section 99 itself permits (s. 99(13)). The power can also be extended by provision in the mortgage, but such extensions are unusual (s. 99(14)). The reason for the exclusion of the statutory power is to prevent the mortgagor using the power for the creation of tenancies which might be protected by the Rent Act, and which could bind the mortgagee, and thus prevent him exercising his rights against the security—*e.g.* by entry into possession and a sale under the statutory power with vacant possession. It has been held that the exclusion of the power of leasing will be effective to enable a mortgagee to evict the illicit tenant. In *Dudley and District Benefit Building Society* v. *Emerson* [1949] Ch. 707 the defendant mortgaged his dwellinghouse to the plaintiff building society; thereafter he purported to grant a weekly tenancy to a Mr. Goodlad, despite the fact that the mortgage contained a clause (usual in Building Society mortgages) excluding the statutory power of leasing, by the mortgagor in possession. When the mortgagor fell into arrears the Building Society commenced proceedings for possession of the mortgaged premises; Mr. Goodlad claimed the protection of the Rent Act. There was no doubt that if his tenancy had been validly granted it would have fallen within the Rent Act. The Court of Appeal, reversing Vaisey J. at first instance, held that the tenancy was not binding on the mortgagee and that therefore the mortgagee was entitled to possession.

In some cases the statutory power cannot be excluded. It cannot, in particular, be excluded in any mortgage of agricultural land made after March 1, 1948 (Agricultural Holdings Act 1948, 7th Schedule; see also *Rhodes* v. *Dalby* [1971] 1 W.L.R. 1325). Likewise, in respect of a lease executed under section 36(4) of the Landlord and Tenant Act 1954 (business premises) the statutory power cannot be excluded.

Even though the statutory power is excluded, however, a tenancy binding on the mortgagee may be created if the mortgagor grants a lease which the mortgagee then proceeds to "adopt." In *Chatsworth Properties Ltd.* v. *Effiom* [1971] 1 W.L.R. 144 a maisonette was mortgaged to the plaintiff company by the mortgagors. The mortgage contained a clause which excluded the statutory power of granting leases. Despite this clause, the mortgagors granted a weekly tenancy of part of the premises to Mr. Effiom. After a default by the mortgagors, the mortgagee exercised his statutory power of appointing a receiver (see *supra*, p. 75) and the solicitors for the mortgagee wrote to Mr. Effiom and directed him to pay his rent to the receiver. Although a receiver is normally the agent of the mortgagor (Law of Property Act s. 109(2), *supra*, p. 76) and the mere receipt of rent by a receiver, being an act on behalf of the mortgagor, cannot bind a mortgagee, it was held by the Court of Appeal that the mortgagee had adopted the tenancy. Mr. Effiom, it was said, on reading the letter from the solicitors to the mortgagee, might reasonably suppose from that letter that the mortgagee had now supplanted the mortgagors as his landlord. Accordingly, it was held that the tenancy was now binding on the mortgagee.

It is probable that if the letter from the solicitors to the tenant had made it clear that the receiver had been appointed by the mortgagee *as mortgagee*, and that no tenancy would be created as between the mortgagee and the tenant by the payment of rent to the receiver, the court would have held that there had been no adoption of the tenancy by the mortgagee and thus the tenancy would not have been binding on the mortgagee (see also *Stroud Building Society* v. *Delamont* [1960] 1 W.L.R. 431).

In many cases, the mortgage will not only contain a clause excluding the statutory power of leasing under section 99 of the Law of Property Act, but also a clause which makes any letting by the mortgagor a breach of his obligations under the mortgage; such a breach will of course make exercisable certain of the powers of a mortgagee (*e.g.* the power of sale). It is clear that such a clause is necessary from the decision in *Iron Trades Employers Assurance Association Ltd.* v. *Union Land and House Investors Ltd.* [1937] Ch. 313 where

Farwell J. held that a lease by a mortgagor would not *per se* constitute a breach of the terms of the mortgage, even though the statutory power of leasing had been excluded. As a result, many standard form mortgages today, such as those used by Building Societies and institutional lenders, contain a clause which makes a letting a breach of the mortgagor's obligations.

The operation of such a "breach" clause was considered in the recent case of *Rhodes* v. *Dalby* [1971] 1 W.L.R. 1325. In that case the court made it clear that the remedy which the mortgagee is claiming is basically similar to a forfeiture and such a clause will be strictly construed. In that case, the plaintiff, as mortgagee, was claiming possession of a farm and premises near Pateley Bridge. The farm had been mortgaged to the plaintiff by the defendant Dalby. The mortgage purported to exclude the statutory power of leasing under section 99, but it was held by the court that this purported exclusion of the statutory power was ineffective because of the provisions of Schedule 7 of the Agricultural Holdings Act 1948 (*supra*, p. 85). The mortgage also contained a clause which provided that the mortgagor should not grant any lease or tenancy of the mortgaged premises or any part thereof without the consent of the mortgagee, and an undertaking by the mortgagee not to enforce his security so long as the mortgagor complied with all his obligations under the mortgage.

The defendant subsequently allowed a Mr. Bush, a teacher in rural studies, to occupy a bungalow on the land. This arrangement was made without the consent of the mortgagee. The arrangement did not, however, constitute a valid lease within section 99 as the "arrangement" did not contain a condition of re-entry on the rent not being paid, as is required by a lease which has been made under section 99(7) of the Law of Property Act. The mortgagee later sought to enforce his security by claiming possession of the farm. It was held that the arrangement between the mortgagor and Mr. Bush was not in fact a breach of the stipulation against letting because the transaction was purely a "gentleman's agreement"; it was thus not legally enforceable and did not constitute a "letting." The inference is that the transaction constituted a licence rather than a lease.

Some types of mortgage, however, go even further than the mortgage in *Rhodes* v. *Dalby*, in that they make it a breach of the obligations of the mortgagor for the mortgagor to grant any lease or tenancy or otherwise part with possession of the mortgaged property. In such a case, the parting with possession even to a licensee (who had exclusive possession) would constitute a breach of the obligations of the mortgagor and would thus render exercisable the remedies of the mortgagee.

2. Insurance

Although a mortgagee is given a statutory power to insure (s. 101) and keep insured the mortgaged property at the expense of the mortgagor, it is not usual to rely on this power as the amount of such insurance is not to exceed the amount allowed by the deed, or, if none is thus allowed, two-thirds of the sum necessary to restore the property after total destruction (s. 108(1)). A mortgage sometimes an express clause requiring the mortgagor to insure the property for its full value; in some cases, a variant is used (especially in Building Society mortgages) which empowers the mortgagee to insure the property to its full value, and to charge the mortgagor with the premiums. The mortgagee may require that insurance moneys received be applied to making good any loss or damage in respect of which it has been paid (s. 108(2), (3)).

3. Redemption

We have seen how the legal right of redemption was strictly construed by the courts of common law, and how this led to equitable intervention, giving the mortgagor an equitable right to redeem. We have also seen how jealously this equitable right to redeem has been safeguarded against contractual interference (*supra*, p. 23). There are however, a few further matters in connection with redemption which should now be considered.

Form

Redemption is basically a process whereby the mortgage is cleared off the title to the property and the mortgagor regains the unencumbered fee simple in the mortgaged property. In former times, when the mortgagee acquired the legal estate in the mortgaged property, it was necessary for the mortgagee to reconvey the property to the mortgagor upon redemption. This is no longer necessary, as the mortgagee no longer acquires the legal estate from the mortgagor, but acquires instead some lesser right in the premises. In the rare cases where the mortgagee does take a legal estate (that is to say, a mortgage by demise) section 116 of the Law of Property Act provides that the mortgage term shall, when the money secured by the mortgage has been discharged, become a satisfied term and shall cease.

The mortgagor will normally require some documentary evidence, however, that the mortgage has been paid off. The Law of Property Act s. 115, provides for an endorsement of the receipt on the mortgage which operates to discharge the mortgaged property from all claims under the mortgage. In the normal way, the receipt will show that the money was paid by the mortgagor. If, however, the receipt records the payment of the mortgage money by a third party (X), the effect of the receipt shall operate as if the benefit of the mortgage had been transferred to the third party (X). In such cases, when a third party has repaid the mortgage debt, it is important to insert in the mortgage receipt a declaration that the receipt is not to operate as a transfer of mortgage.

In the common case where the mortgage debt is repaid by the personal representative of a deceased mortgagor, there is no need for such a provision, as the Act provides that the receipt is not to operate as a transfer where the mortgage is paid off out of capital money, or other money in the hands of a personal representative or trustee properly applicable for the discharge of the mortgage, and it is not expressly provided that the receipt is to operate as a transfer (Law of Property Act s. 115(2)).

Instead of a standard form of vacating receipt, a deed of discharge may be required in some cases, as for instance, when only part of the mortgaged property is being discharged.

In the case of registered land, the procedure is slightly different. Here the mortgage is discharged by a notification in the register that the charge has been cancelled. This means that the land certificate, which has been lodged in the Registry during the currency of the mortgage, will be redelivered to the mortgagor, who is the registered proprietor of the land (Land Registration Act 1925, s. 35).

The statutory process of discharge by vacating receipt is also inapplicable to equitable mortgages. Here it is necessary for the mortgagee to reconvey the interest which he has acquired as a result of the mortgage to the mortgagor. The practice has grown up of accepting a letter from the mortgagee acknowledging that he has no claim in respect of the property, and this procedure is particularly common in cases where (say) a building estate is being developed with the aid of a bank loan secured by an equitable mortgage of the plot, each sub-plot being released from the equitable mortgage on completion of the house and conveyance to the purchaser. This practice is not without its dangers (see 1962 Conv. N.S. 449) but appears to be prevalent.

After redemption, the mortgagee should return the title deeds to the mortgagor; he is under no obligation to search in the Land Charges Register to see if there is a subsequent incumbrance to whom the deeds should be handed. He is required to hand over the deeds to a subsequent mortgagee only if he has notice of his rights, and section 96(2) of the Law of Property Act provides expressly that notice for this purpose does not include statutory notice implied by reason of the Land Charges Act 1972.

In some cases, however, there are particular problems which

arise in connection with the right to redeem and it might be convenient to deal with them here.

Consolidation

Consolidation, essentially, is the right of a mortgagee to insist on simultaneous redemption of multiple mortgages. The rationale of the rule is this. Suppose that A. mortgages two properties, Pinkacre and Blueacre, to M. to secure £10,000 each. At the time of the creation of the mortgage each property was worth £15,000, and so the loans were amply secured. Because of developments in the neighbourhood, the value of Pinkacre declines sharply to £9,000. Now, clearly, in relation to Pinkacre, M. is under-secured. Suppose, however, that Blueacre is blessed with the good fortune which has so conspicuously evaded Pinkacre, and is now worth £30,000. Clearly, if one adds together the values of Blueacre and Pinkacre, M. is adequately secured as the total value of the two properties is (£9,000+£30,000)=£39,000. The total outstanding mortgage debt is (£10,000+£10,000)=£20,000. Clearly, however, if A. was to redeem Blueacre and leave M. holding the Pinkacre baby, M. would find himself under-secured. Hence, equity developed its doctrine of consolidation; the essence of this doctrine is that if A. seeks to redeem Blueacre, he will only be allowed to do so on condition that he redeems the less desirable Pinkacre as well. The right to redeem which is vested in A. is itself a creature of equity; if he seeks to exercise his equitable right to redeem, equity will insist that "he who comes to equity must do equity"; and in this context "doing equity" consists in redeeming the less favoured of the two securities.

Although the rationale of the rule about consolidation is that a mortgagee shall not be left bereft of his security by variation in the value of the mortgaged property, the doctrine of consolidation has now become a technical doctrine which is applicable in such a case whether or not there has been such a dramatic fluctuation in the value of the securities. If certain conditions are satisfied a mortgagee can insist on consolidation regardless of the value of the properties. It will, however, normally be insisted on in the case of such a fluctuation, but proof of such fluctuation is not necessary for a mortgagee who seeks to insist on consolidation. The doctrine is not a particularly attractive one; it seems anomalous that a mortgagee who has selected one of his securities badly should be able to redress the balance by calling upon a mortgagor to redeem it when he seeks to redeem a better security, but the rule is too well entrenched to be challenged. Strict conditions, however, are imposed before the right to insist on consolidation can be exercised. These conditions were formulated in the loading case of *Pledge* v. *White* [1896] A.C. 187, and are as follows:

(a) *Legal date for redemption passed*

In the case of both mortgages, the legal date for redemption must have passed. Before the legal date for redemption has passed, the mortgagor would not be relying upon his equitable right to redeem, and the doctrine of consolidation is essentially an equitable doctrine which operates as a restriction on the equitable right to redeem. Before the legal date for redemption has passed, equity is in no position to impose conditions on redemption at law.

(b) *Right reserved*

The right to insist on consolidation is no longer an automatic right of the mortgagee. Section 93(1) of the Law of Property Act provides

> "A mortgagor seeking to redeem any one mortgage is entitled to do so without paying any money due under any separate mortgage made by him, or by any person through whom he claims, solely on property other than that comprised in the mortgage which he seeks to redeem.
>
> "This subsection applies only if and so far as a contrary intention is not expressed in the mortgage deeds or one of them."

It might be added that the reservation of such a right to insist on consolidation is usual.

(c) *Same mortgagor*

Both mortgagees in respect of which consolidation is sought must have been made by the same mortgagor.

(d) *Union of equities and mortgages*

There must have been a moment in time when both mortgages were vested in the same person as mortgagee, and both equities in the same person as mortgagor.

(e) *Same mortgagee seeking to enforce*

At the time when consolidation is sought to be imposed, the mortgages must be in the hands of the same person. Consolidation can only occur when, at the moment when redemption is sought, the mortgagee is also entitled *as mortgagee* to another mortgage. We have seen that there must at some point have been a union in one hand of both mortgages and both equities; a subsequent separation of the equities will not prevent consolidation, but subsequent separation of the mortgages into different hands will.

The operation of these rules can best be illustrated by a number of examples:

Example (i)

A.————M.1.
A.————M.2.————M.1.

This diagram represents the following stages. It is assumed that conditions (1) and (2) above are satisfied.

1. A. mortgages the first property to M.1.

2. A. mortgages the second property to M.2.
3. M.2. transfers his mortgage to M.1.

Here consolidation is possible, as all conditions are satisfied.

Example (*ii*)

```
A.————M.1. }
A.————M.2. } T.
```

1. A. mortgages the first property to M.1.
2. A. mortgages the second property to M.2.
3. M.1. transfers his mortgage to T.
4. M.2. transfers his mortgage to T.

Again, consolidation is possible.

Example (*iii*)

```
B.
|
A.————M.1. }
A.————M.2. } T.
```

1. A. mortgages the first property to M.1.
2. A. mortgages the second property to M.2.
3. A. transfers the equity of redemption on the first mortgage to B.
4. M.1. transfers his mortgage to T.
5. M.2. transfers his mortgage to T.

Here consolidation is not possible; condition (d) above is not satisfied, as the equities became separated into different hands before the union of mortgages in T.

Example (*iv*)

```
A.————M.1. }
B.————M.2. } T.
|
A.
```

1. A. mortgages the first property to M.1.
2. B. mortgages the second property to M.2.
3. M.1. transfers his mortgage to T.
4. M.2. transfers his mortgage to T.
5. B. transfers the equity of redemption in his mortgage to A.

Here, no consolidation is possible, despite the fact that the mortgages are concentrated in one hand (T.) and both equities are now in the hands of A. Condition (c), which requires both mortgages to have been made by the same mortgagor, is not satisfied.

Example (*v*)

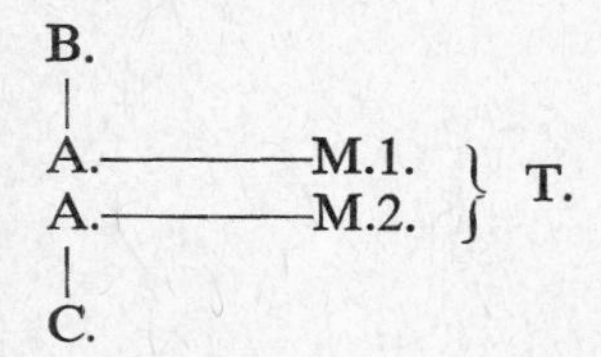

1. A. mortgages the first property to M.1.
2. A. mortgages the second property to M.2.
3. M.1. transfers his mortgage to T.
4. M.2. transfers his mortgage to T.
5. A. transfers the equity of redemption on the first mortgage to B.
6. A. transfers the equity of redemption on the second mortgage to C.

Here, consolidation is possible, as all five conditions are satisfied. The doctrine is clearly something of a hazard in this case to a purchaser of the equity of redemption, such as B. If C. attempted to redeem the second mortgage, B. might find himself, to his surprise, compelled to redeem as well. At the time of his purchase of the equity of redemption, B. might well be unaware of the fact that A. had made a mortgage on other property in favour of M.2. In fact, he would very likely be in ignorance of the whole affair, since the mortgage relating to the second property would be with the deeds relating to the second property; B., as a purchaser of the equity of redemption of the first property would not be likely to see the deeds relating to the second property. It seems particularly hard that a purchaser without notice should have to pay the penalty for the mortgagee's imprudence as a lender.

The doctrine applies whether the mortgages are legal or equitable; it has even been held that the doctrine applies to two mortgages in respect of the same property. In *Re Salmon* [1903] 1 K.B. 147, before his decline into bankruptcy, a mortgagor granted three successive mortgages to M.1., M.2., and M.3. After the mortgagor became bankrupt, M.1., the first mortgagee, took transfers from the second and third mortgages from M.2. and M.3. respectively. The position was thus as follows:

S.————M.1.
S.————M.2. }
S.————M.3. } M.1.

The trustee in bankruptcy of the mortgagor sought to redeem the first mortgage (that is to say the mortgage originally granted to M.1.). M.1. was unwilling to allow him to do so unless he also redeemed the other mortgages at the same time. These were the mortgages which had originally been created in favour of M.2. and M.3., but to which M.1. had become entitled to transfer. It was held by the court that M.1. could insist on consolidation in these circumstances. The case seems very odd, and it is difficult to see how the case can be reconciled with the rationale of the doctrine of consolidation. We have seen that the whole basis of the doctrine of consolidation is to enable a mortgagee to resist the imperilling of his security by redemption by the mortgagor. Now, in *Re Salmon,* when the first mortgage (the mortgage to M.1.) was redeemed, it is difficult to see how the security of the second and third mortgages can be said to be imperilled. On the contrary, their security will be enhanced, because they will now rank higher in order of priority, with the first mortgage out of the way.

Redeem up foreclose down

This rather mysterious maxim applies in cases where there are multiple mortgages. We have hitherto used the term "redemption" to describe the process whereby a mortgagor recovers his property from the hands of a mortgagee. It is, however, also applicable to describe the process whereby a later mortgagee "buys up" the place in the queue of a higher mortgagee by redeeming his mortgage. The maxim only applies if formal redemption by action in court (which is itself unusual) is necessary. Suppose, for instance, that property has been mortgaged as follows:

M.————A. £5,000
M.————B. £1,000
M.————C. £1,000
M.————D. £1,000
M.————E. £500

D., prima facie, ranks fourth in order of priority, and he may feel that he is rather too low in the batting order for comfort, especially if the property is declining in value and may well be insufficient to satisfy mortgagees who are as low down as he is. Now, if D. could acquire B's place in the order (*i.e.* second in the queue—or first wicket down) he would be in a better position. To do so, he will have to pay off B., (*i.e.* redeem him) by paying to B. the amount due on his mortgage, (£1,000) but D. may feel that the price is worth paying as he will gain a better position for priority. In a case as complex as this, it is probably necessary that proceedings in court will have to be taken, as there will clearly be some complex accounts to disentangle.

Now, C. is affected by this: if D.'s claim to redeem B. is successful, C. will find his chances of recovering anything affected, since his chances of regaining his investment clearly depend upon the amount which turns out to be due to B. Accordingly, *as a rule of procedure*, C. must be made a party to the action too, and this can only be done by D. taking redemption proceedings against him also. In addition, it gives *locus standi* to apply for a judicial sale, under section 91(2) of the Law of Property Act 1925. Hence the first part of the rule: if a mortgagee seeks to redeem, by action, a prior mortgagee, he must also redeem, in the same action, any mortgagees who rank for priority between his own mortgage and the mortgage of which redemption is sought. Now, whilst the accounts between B., C., and D. are being settled, it seems only reasonable that an attempt be made, once and for all, to clear up the accounts in respect of other incumbrancers interested in the equity of redemption, namely E., the subsequent mortgagee, and M., the mortgagor. To clear up their accounts, it is important that E. and M. be made parties to the proceedings also; this can only be done by foreclosure; hence the rule is that mortgagees ranking below the mortgagee seeking to redeem the higher mortgagee must be made parties to the action by foreclosure, as must the mortgagor himself. Hence, *foreclose down*. It will be observed that there is no necessity to make A., the first mortgagee a party to the action. His priority will not be affected, as he will remain, in any event, first in the queue for purposes of priority.

Note

[1] See also, Megarry and Wade, p. 926; Cheshire, p. 650; Waldock, p. 215; Nokes, p. 57; Fisher and Lightwood, p. 293.

CHAPTER 7

PRIORITY OF MORTGAGES[1]

THIS is a complex topic, which has surprisingly been very little litigated since 1925, when the rules as to priority were radically reshaped. The scarcity of litigation on the topic is all the more surprising when one contemplates the new rules and the dreadful uncertainty that surrounds them in many places (see Megarry 7 C.L.J. 249).

The problem arises in this way. If a plot of land is mortgaged to a number of mortgagees in such a way that the value of the property is unable to satisfy the claims of all the mortgagees, there is no question of all the mortgagees sharing equally in the common disaster, each receiving a proportion of his loan. The rule is that the order of priority of the several mortgagees must be determined, and the first in priority paid in full before anything is given to those who rank below him in priority.

Before 1926, a series of complex rules had been evolved for dealing with questions of priority between competing mortgagees. These rules were in general, an expression of the normal rules of priority between competing legal and equitable interests, although, as we shall see, the rules were modified in certain circumstances for no very discernible reasons. As a result of the 1925 legislation, these rules have been to some extent eradicated, and the primary question which has to be asked is a different one. The question, in case of unregistered land, is now generally one concerning the application of the Land Charges Act, since some mortgages are now registrable under the provisions of that Act. In the case of registered land, a different set of rules seem to apply, considerably complicated by the fact that there are so many different ways of making a mortgage of registered land. To complicate matters even further, there is the problem of the continued survival, in a number of cases, of the rules which applied before 1925. In this account, a break will be made with usual custom, and no attempt will be made to explain the pre-1926 rules as a kind of grisly prelude; an attempt will be made to deal with such parts of the pre-1926 rules as are relevant in the appropriate place.

It may be asked why questions of priority, which were frequently litigated before 1926, have been so little agitated in the courts since that date, despite the encouragement which the obscure provisions of the Property legislation might appear to give to the litigious. The answer probably lies in the relatively rapid increase in property values which has taken place in the last half-century and particularly in the last decade. A priority question only normally becomes relevant when there is insufficient for all the mortgagees to be satisfied in full. With rapidly increasing property values, even if a property is (initially) overmortgaged, things may well cure themselves within a relatively short time so that the property becomes worth enough to satisfy all the mortgagees in full. Some of the main problems have arisen with regard to registered land; but the main difficulties in that area have concerned the priority of mortgages with regard to the holders of minor interests created after the mortgage, rather than a problem of priority *inter se* of mortgagees.

1. Mortgages of Unregistered Land

The basic principle here is first come, first served: in other words, mortgages prima facie rank for priority in order of their creation. We shall see however, that this principle may sometimes be disturbed by the operation of the Land Charges Act 1972, which may have the effect of rendering a prior registrable but unregistered mortgage void against a subsequent purchaser (Land Charges Act 1972, s. 4); a purchaser, for this purpose, includes a mortgagee (Land Charges Act 1972, s. 17(1)). The basic order of priority (first in time) may also be disturbed by the survival of some of the pre-1926 rules as to priority, which in some cases preferred a second mortgagee to a first mortgagee where the first mortgagee's conduct made it inequitable for him to claim the priority that would have been his by priority of creation.

An initial enquiry, then, must be directed to the question of "when is a mortgage registrable under the Land Charges Act?" The key sections of the Act are those sections that define a *puisne mortgage* (s. 2(4)(i)) and a *general equitable charge* (s. 2(4)(iii)).

Section 2(4)(i) of the Land Charges Act 1972 provides as follows:

> "A puisne mortgage is a legal mortgage which is not protected by a deposit of documents relating to the legal estate affected."

Section 2(4)(iii) of the same act provides:

> "A general equitable charge is any equitable charge which—
>
> (a) is not secured by a deposit of documents relating to the legal estate affected; and
>
> (b) does not arise or affect an interest arising under a trust for sale or a settlement; and
>
> (c) is not a charge given by way of indemnity against rents equitably apportioned or charged exclusively on land in exoneration of other land and against the breach or non-observance of covenants or conditions; and
>
> (d) is not included in any other class of land charge."

It seems that the definition of a puisne mortgage is clear enough, in that it comprehends *legal* mortgages not protected by deposit of deeds. The definition of a general equitable charge, consisting as it does of a resounding series of negatives, is rather less easy to understand, but it is generally taken to include all species of equitable mortgages which are not protected by deposit of deeds. Thus far, all seems tolerably clear, in that all mortgages not protected by deposit of deeds are registrable as land charges; if legal, they fall within section

2(4)(i), and if equitable within class 2(4)(iii).

Problems, however, remain. What is meant by the seemingly innocuous expression "not protected by a deposit of documents relating to the legal estate affected?" Suppose a mortgagor creates a mortgage in favour of a mortgagee and deposits his title deeds with him. The mortgage is clearly then protected by a deposit of deeds and is not registrable. The mortgagor then persuades the mortgagee to hand the documents back to him on some pretext or another—a desire to check one's boundaries being a favourite one which at least has the merit of antiquity (see *The Thatched House* case, *infra*, p. 105, and the other cases mentioned under "recovery and redeposit" below). Does the mortgage then cease to be protected by deposit of deeds and thus become registrable? If the mortgagor then returns the deeds, after checking his boundaries, or whatever, does the mortgage become unregistrable again? Does the mortgage have to live a kind of Cheshire Cat existence, entering and leaving the Land Charges Register as often as the mortgagor "borrows" his deeds back and returns them?

There are no clear answers to these questions. The general opinion seems to be that the Act should be read as if it read "*originally* protected by deposit ..." (see Megarry, 7 C.L.J. 243). Otherwise, there is a risk of the Land Register becoming cluttered with a number of registrations of charges which are destined to be removed again in a relatively short time. To hold such a mortgage to be unregistrable, even if the mortgagee has parted with the possession of the mortgage deeds, has the corresponding disadvantage that it renders relevant yet again the pre-1926 rules as to priority, which as we shall see, remain relevant between competing mortgagees both of whose interests are protected by deposit of deeds. The uncertainty could be serious; the penalties for a wrong guess about the applicability of the Land Charges Act are drastic in the extreme, as the plaintiffs in *Shiloh Spinners Ltd.* v. *Harding* [1972] Ch. 326 found out to their cost, when they failed to register an interest which they pardonably assumed to be unregistrable, but which was held by the Court of

Appeal (but not the House of Lords) to be capable of registration (see 1971 C.L.J. 258, [1973] 2 W.L.R. 28). It will be assumed in the following account, although without any confidence on the part of the author, that the traditional view that a mortgage does not become registrable by the mortgagee parting with the deeds is the correct one.

The difficulties do not end there; it was suggested above that equitable mortgages not protected by deposit of deeds were registrable as general equitable charges; equitable mortgages protected by deposit of deeds were not registrable at all, the logic of this being that the absence of the title deeds would constitute notice of the existence of the prior mortgage. Further consideration, however, suggests that both these assertions are open to challenge.

First, it might be argued that an equitable mortgage, even if protected by deposit of deeds, is registrable as a class C(iv) land charge (estate contract), within section 2(4)(iv) of the Land Charges Act 1972. An estate contract is defined as "a contract by an estate owner or by a person entitled at the date of the contract to have a legal estate conveyed to him to convey or create a legal estate. . . ." Now, it was observed above that most equitable mortgages derive their validity from the application of the well-known doctrine of *Walsh* v. *Lonsdale* (1882) 21 Ch. D. 9 to mortgages. An equitable mortgage in fact arises from the willingness of a court of equity to grant specific performance of a contract to create a mortgage. An equitable mortgage, like our old friend the equitable lease, thus constitutes a contract "to convey or create a legal estate" and is registrable in class C(iv). The argument is logically compelling, but would be profoundly disconcerting in practice if it proved to be correct. It is not customary to register as Land Charges equitable mortgages protected by deposit of deeds, and, if such mortgages were to begin to be held void for non-registration, banks, at least, would be in for some unpleasant surprises. The only way out of the dilemma is to hold, as Megarry & Wade suggest (p. 964) that equitable mortgages by deposit of deeds are now an independent kind of interest in land, no longer dependent on the doctrine of *Walsh* v. *Lonsdale* for their validity (see also Wolstenholme & Cherry, Vol. II, p. 18; Cheshire, p. 684).

As if this was not enough, it is also possible to argue that equitable mortgages *not* protected by deposit of deeds are *not* registrable as general equitable charges either. This rather unexpected conclusion (which leaves little apparent function for class C(iii)) is based on the following argument. Section 2(4)(iii) of the Land Charges Act 1972 (which defines the general equitable charge) is basically a residual class of land charge. It includes an equitable charge "which is not included in any other class of land charge." If the argument outlined above is correct, and equitable mortgages derive their validity from the application of the rule in *Walsh* v. *Lonsdale* to a contract to create a mortgage, it would seem that in principle all equitable mortgages, including those not protected by deposit of deeds, should fall within section 2(4)(iv) of the Act (estate contract). If they do, then of course an equitable mortgage is not registrable as a general equitable charge, as it now is included in another class of land charge. The point may be important, as the effect of failure to register may depend on which type of land charge has not been registered. An unregistered charge in class C(iii) (general equitable charge) is void against a purchaser for value of any interest in the land (legal or equitable); a charge in class C(iv) (estate contract) is void *only* against a purchaser for *money or money's worth* of a *legal estate* in the land. (Land Charges Act 1972, s. 4(5), (6)). It will be assumed hereafter, again with the minimum of confidence that unprotected equitable mortgages are registrable within section 2(4)(iii) of the Land Charges Act (general equitable charge) and not section 2(4)(iv) (estate contract).

Assuming that the reader has not been sufficiently dismayed by this stage to give up the topic altogether, there appear to be four possible situations of fact:

(a) Both mortgages protected by deposit.
(b) First mortgage protected, second unprotected.
(c) First mortgage unprotected, second protected.

(d) Neither mortgage protected.

These situations will now be considered in turn.

(a) Both mortgages protected by deposit

This is not as improbable as it sounds. It is suggested that the situation could arise in the following two situations:

(i) Division of deeds. The mortgagor might deposit some of his deeds with the first mortgagee, A., and some with the second mortgagee, B. In *Lacon* v. *Allen* (1856) 3 Drew. 579; 61 E.R. 1024, a mortgagor deposited some of his deeds with Allen, the first mortgagor, and retained others. These retained documents he later deposited with Lacon, his banker, as security for a loan. It was assumed by the court (though the point was not particularly relevant) that both mortgages should be regarded as protected by deposit of deeds.

(ii) Recovery and redeposit. The mortgagor might deposit all his deeds with A., the first mortgagee; he might then recover them on some pretext or another and then hand them over to a second mortgagee. Thus, in the *Thatched House* case (*Peter* v. *Russel*) (1716) 1 Ec. Ca. Abr. 321 one Goff mortgaged the Thatched House at St. James to a Dr. Lancaster and deposited the deeds with him. He afterwards recovered the deeds from the mortgagee on the pretext that he wished to check the area of the premises, and deposited them with the plaintiff, the second mortgagee, as security for a loan. Likewise, in *Northern Counties of England Fire Insurance Co.* v. *Whipp* (1884) 26 Ch. D. 482, one Crabtree, who was the manager of the plaintiff company, mortgaged the property to the company and placed the deeds in the company safe. As manager to the company, he had a key to the safe. He used the key to abstract the deeds from the safe, and then deposited them with Whipp as security for a loan. It is suggested that in both these cases today, the first and second mortgages would, on the analysis above, be regarded as protected by deposit of deeds.

If one has a conflict between mortgagees, both protected by deposit, the property legislation of 1925 gives little help. The only section which appears to be relevant is section 13 of the Law of Property Act, which provides (unhelpfully):

> "This Act shall not prejudicially affect the right or interest of any person arising out of or consequent on the possession by him of any documents relating to a legal estate in land, nor affect any question arising out of or consequent upon any omission to obtain or any other absence of possession by any person of any documents relating to a legal estate in land."

In other words, back to square one—the rules before 1926. These rules depended for their operation on whether the mortgages in question were legal or equitable. There are again four possible situations of fact:

(i) Both mortgages legal
(ii) First mortgage legal, second mortgage equitable
(iii) First mortgage equitable, second mortgage legal
(iv) Both mortgages equitable.

(i) *Both mortgages legal*

Here the pre-1926 cases are of very little help, as there was little possibility of the creation of successive legal mortgages before 1926. The first mortgage would vest the legal estate in the first mortgagee, and so there would be no opportunity for the creation of successive legal mortgages. The only way in which successive legal mortgages could have been created before 1926 was by the creation of successive legal terms of years, and few problems concerning priority between successive legal mortgagees seem to have troubled the courts.

Since 1925, however, when mortgages take effect by demise, sub-demise, or charge, there is no obstacle to the creation of a succession of legal mortgages. If a question of priority arose, it is likely that the first in time would prevail as a general rule. It is probable however that the first mortgagee could lose his priority by his misconduct—if he was guilty of fraud, misrepresentation, or gross negligence. These problems usually arise in connection with situation (ii) *infra*, and will be more fully discussed in that context.

(ii) *First mortgage legal, second equitable*

Here, on two grounds, one would expect the legal mortgagee to prevail. He is first in time, and his possession of a legal interest should entitle him to priority, all things being equal, over a mere equitable incumbrancer. However, the legal mortgagee's misconduct might stop all things being equal; and in the many cases of this type which came before the courts before 1926, it was well established that if the legal mortgages had been guilty of fraud, estoppel, or gross negligence, he was liable to be postponed (*i.e.* lose his priority to) a later equitable mortgagee.

(a) Fraud. If the first (legal) mortgagee was party to a scheme whereby the mortgagor was enabled fraudulently to misrepresent the property to the second equitable mortgagee as unencumbered, he would lose his priority in favour of the equitable mortgagee. In the *Thatched House* case (*supra*) it was said "if a man makes a mortgage, and afterwards mortgages the same estate to another, and the first mortgagee is in combination to induce the second mortgagee to lend his money, this fraud without doubt will in Equity postpone his own mortgage." It was found on the facts that there was no fraud in that case, but this dictum was approved in the later case of *Northern Counties Fire Insurance* v. *Whipp* (*supra*).

(b) Estoppel. The rule here has certain similarities to the doctrine of estoppel in the law relating to the transfer of property by a non-owner in the Sale of Goods (*cf.* Sale of Goods Act 1893, s. 21). If the legal mortgagee by word or conduct allows the mortgagor to deal with the property as if it was unencumbered, he will lose his priority to a later equitable mortgagee. Thus, in *Rimmer* v. *Webster* [1902] 2 Ch. 163 (a contest between two equitable mortgagees) the first mortgagee allowed it to appear that the first mortgage had been paid off when this was not in fact the case. Thus the mortgagor was allowed to represent to the second mortgagee that the property was in fact unencumbered. Again, in *Perry-Herrick* v. *Attwood* (1857) 2 De G. & J. 21, Attwood raised some money by way of a legal mortgage, but was allowed to retain the title deeds for the purpose of raising further loans on the security of the property. It was held that the first mortgagee was postponed to the second mortgagee, who lent his money without notice of the rights of the first mortgagee. Lord Cranforth L.C. said "If a person taking a legal mortgage chooses to leave the deeds with the mortgagor, not through negligence or through fraud, but with the intention of enabling him to raise a sum of £15,000, which is to take precedence of the legal mortgage, the mortgagee cannot, as against subsequent incumbrancers complain, if, instead of £15,000, the mortgagee raises £50,000 because he himself put it into his power to raise any sum he pleases."

(c) Gross negligence in relation to the title deeds. This gives rise to difficulties. There is authority to suggest that mere carelessness is not enough (*Northern Counties etc.* v. *Whipp*, *supra*, p. 105), though it is difficult to see how the addition of the epithet "gross" to the concept of negligence makes any real difference. To confuse matters further, it appears to be relevant to enquire whether the mortgagee's negligence was in relation to his failure to obtain the deeds or his failure to retain them.

(1) *Failure to obtain.* In the puzzling case of *Walker* v. *Linom* [1907] 2 Ch. 104, a purchaser who failed to obtain all the deeds from his transferor (leaving the most recent deed in his possession) was postponed to a subsequent equitable mortgagee who scarcely appears to have investigated title

at all. The application of the law to the facts is odd, but the principle seems correct. One would expect a subsequent equitable mortgagee to gain priority only if he has exercised due diligence, and it is difficult to see how this could be said of the mortgagee in *Walker* v. *Linom*. A legal mortgagee who fails to make any attempt to obtain the deeds will certainly lose his priority (*Colyer* v. *Finch* (1856) 5 H.L.C. 905); but it seems that if the legal mortgagee accepts a remarkably feeble excuse for non-production of the deeds, he will not lose priority. (See *Manners* v. *Mew* (1885) 29 Ch. D. 725, where the mortgagee was simply told that "the matter had slipped the mortgagor's memory.")

(2) *Failure to retain.* In the unsatisfactory case of *Northern Counties of England Fire Insurance Co.* v. *Whipp*, the facts of which have already been given (*supra*, p. 105), it was held that the company, as first (legal) mortgagee, did not lose their priority, even though they had allowed the mortgagor to have a key to the safe where the deeds were kept. It might be thought that this was as clear a case of gross negligence as could be imagined. The court, however, held that the legal mortgagee had retained his priority, and it may be that in the case of a failure to *retain* the deeds only negligence of an even grosser kind than in the "obtaining" cases will suffice. The judgment, however, abounds with unhelpful phrases like "negligence so gross as to amount to fraud." The dicta in the case are sweeping enough to comprehend a failure to obtain the deeds as well as a failure to retain them, and they appear to be contrary to the decision of the House of Lords in *Colyer* v. *Finch* (*supra*). Many textwriters believe that a grossly negligent failure to *retain* the deeds should be a ground for loss of priority; Waldock, (p. 39) for instance, argues that the decision in *Whipp*'s case is unsupportable because it is heavily reliant upon the notion of constructive fraud in equity, which was rejected by the House of Lords a few years later in *Derry* v. *Peek* (1889) 14 A.C. 337.

(iii) *First mortgage equitable, second legal*

Here, prima facie, one would expect the problem of priority to be solved by recourse to the general principle of equity. As between competing incumbrancers, it is usually said that a prior equitable incumbrance binds any subsequent purchaser except a bona fide purchaser for value of a legal estate without notice, actual, constructive, or imputed (*Pilcher* v. *Rawlins* (1872) 7 Ch. App. 259). On principle, therefore, it seems that a subsequent legal mortgage should not gain priority over a prior equitable mortgagee unless he is such a bona fide purchaser. General principles of constructive notice would require the legal mortgagee to make such enquiries into the title as a prudent mortgagee would make.

Despite this clear principle, however, the cases suggest that the true rule is slightly different. So long as the legal mortgagee is not guilty of gross negligence, he will take priority. This appears to be a case where the concept of gross negligence has been translated from situation (ii) (postponement of a prior legal mortgagee to a later equitable mortgagee) where it has a legitimate role to play, to a totally different situation where it is downright confusing. Why a later legal mortgagee should be allowed to prevail over an earlier equitable mortgagee without having to shoulder the heavy burden of proof which normally rests upon any person claiming to be a bona fide purchaser seems incomprehensible. Incomprehensible or not, the cases seem to establish the rule clearly, even though the doctrine of constructive notice almost disappears to vanishing point. Thus in *Hewitt* v. *Loosemore* (1851) 9 Hare 449, Robert Loosemore, a solicitor, deposited a lease with Hewitt, the plaintiff, as security for a loan, thus creating an equitable mortgage. He subsequently granted a legal mortgage to John Loosemore, a farmer who "was unacquainted with legal forms." His acquaintance was sufficiently nodding, however, for him to ask Robert Loosemore "whether the lease of the premises ought not to be delivered to him as well." Robert replied "that it should, but that as he was rather busy then, he would look for it and give it to the defendant when he next came to market." Despite his uncritical acceptance or this rather flimsy tale, John Loosemore was held to take priority over Hewitt as he had not been guilty of gross negligence. Likewise, in *Agra Bank* v. *Barry* (1874) L.R. 7 H.L. 135 an excuse for non-production of deeds "that they were at the mortgagor's residence in Ireland" was held insufficient to entitle a prior equitable mortgagee by deposit to prevail over a subsequent gullible legal mortgagee who accepted the excuse.

This anomalous doctrine of gross negligence ought only to apply, if at all, as between competing mortgagees; but in *Oliver* v. *Hinton* [1899] 2 Ch. 264 it was even applied to a purchaser of the legal estate, who, it was said, took subject to a prior equitable mortgage because of his "gross negligence." This case seems extraordinary; it would have been far simpler to hold the purchaser bound on the straightforward principle that he had failed to show that he was a bona fide purchaser for value of a legal estate without notice, actual or constructive.

(iv) *Both mortgages equitable*

Here, prima facie, the first in time prevails. Again, however, it seems that the mortgagee who was prior in time might lose his priority on the ground of fraud estoppel, or gross negligence. Thus, in *Rimmer* v. *Webster* (*supra*, p. 108) an equitable mortgagee who was prior in time was postponed to a later equitable mortgagee because the first mortgagee had by his conduct allowed the mortgagor to appear to be the unencumbered owner of the property.

(b) First mortgage protected, second unprotected

Here, the general principle is easy to discern. The first mortgagee will usually take priority, because he is first in time. It is possible, however, that he might forfeit his priority if he was guilty of fraud, estoppel, or gross negligence (*e.g.* by failure to retain the deeds—subject to *Whipp*'s case, *supra*, p. 105). Section 13 of the Law of Property Act (quoted above, p. 106) seems to retain the old rules of priority concerning custody or non-custody of title deeds.

Another possible complication arises when the first mortgage, protected by deposit, is equitable and the second mortgage legal. We have seen that the doctrine of notice in its usual form does not apply here—or, at any rate, if it does apply, a different interpretation must be given to the idea of "constructive notice" from that which usually obtains. It has been suggested that if the second mortgagee, having taken without notice of the prior mortgage, were to register his mortgage as a puisne mortgage (section 2(4)(i) of the Land Charges Act 1972) he might lose the priority which is prima facie his as a purchaser without notice, because of the impact of section 97 of the Law of Property Act 1925. This section provides, in effect, that the registered mortgage shall rank for priority according to its date of *registration*, which, *ex hypothesi*, is later than the date of *creation* of the first mortgage (see Megarry, 7 C.L.J. 258). The inconvenience of suggestion is manifest, as Megarry himself admits; his suggestion that section 97 is irrelevant, because the second (legal) mortgagee has already *obtained* his priority by virtue of purchase without notice, seems, with respect, to be convincing.

(c) First mortgage not protected, second protected

Here again, the solution seems relatively simple, as section 4 of the Land Charges Act 1972 appears to govern the situation. The first mortgage is necessarily registrable (as a puisne mortgage or a general equitable charge). If so registered, the registration will constitute *actual* notice (Law of Property Act, s. 198) to all persons and for all purposes, and so a later mortgagee will take subject to the prior mortgage.

There is however a suggestion that section 13 of the Law of Property Act might in certain circumstances prevent section 198 from having its usual effect. The provisions of this section have already been quoted (see p. 106). Megarry (*loc. cit.*) argues that a prior legal mortgagee who was grossly negligent in failing to obtain the title deeds (*cf. Walker* v. *Linom* (*supra*, p. 108)) but who later registered his mortgage might not be able to claim the priority which section 198 appears to accord to him, because section 13 has preserved the old rule about custody or non-custody of title deeds. The awkwardness of the suggestion is recognised by Megarry himself, and a solution might be found by recognising that the second mortgagee would have failed to make the enquiries a prudent man should make, since he had not searched the Land Charges Register and he would have constructive notice of all that such a search would reveal. He could not thus claim his priority under section 13, as he had not himself taken all the steps needed to gain (or preserve) priority.

If, on the other hand, the first mortgagee has failed to register, section 4 of the Land Charges Act seems to solve the problem conclusively as it renders the unregistered mortgage void against a purchaser (including a mortgagee) of any interest (legal or equitable) in the land. Actual notice of the prior mortgage would not affect the position of the second mortgagee since notice is irrelevant (Law of Property Act s. 199; *Hollington Bros.* v. *Rhodes* [1951] W.N. 437).

(d) Neither mortgage protected

Here, by definition both mortgages are registrable. There are two statutory sections which appear to apply. They are (i) section 97 of the Law of Property Act, which provides that registrable mortgages shall rank according to their date of registration; and (ii) section 4 of the Land Charges Act, 1972, which provides that an unregistered mortgage shall be void against a purchaser (including a mortgagee) of a legal or equitable interest in the land.

The operation of these sections depends to some extent upon the facts. In the following examples, it is assumed that the mortgages are created in the order *A. first, B. second*, and that both mortgages are registrable.

EXAMPLE (i)

A. registers before B.'s mortgage is created
Here, section 198 would seem to accord priority, in all circumstances, to A.

EXAMPLE (ii)

B. registers, then A. registers
Again, the solution seems clear. B. should prevail on two grounds:

(a) A.'s mortgage was void against him for want of registration (Land Charges Act 1972, s. 4(5)).
(b) the mortgages rank for priority in order of *registration*, which was B., A. (Law of Property Act section 97).

The result is clear, but it is not easy to see why two statutory sections should be needed to do the work of one. This prompts the suspicion that one or other of them is redundant; this suspicion becomes relevant later.

EXAMPLE (iii)

A. registers after the creation of B.'s mortgage; B. does not register at all
Here there are difficulties (Megarry, *op. cit.*, p. 258). Section 4 of the Land Charges Act clearly gives B. priority, for A.'s mortgage was void against him; but B.'s eventual registration (if any) must take place after A.'s, so that section would appear to accord priority to A. The answer probably, is that section 97 only comes into play when both mortgages are registered. In B.'s case, since no registration takes place, it is the date of *creation* that matters, and *at that date*, A.'s mortgage was void against him. So the order is B., A.

EXAMPLE (iv)

B. registers, A. does not

Again, problems arise. The Land Charges Act clearly accords priority to B., since A.'s mortgage was void against him at the date of creation. The suggestion advanced above (Example (iii)) that section 97 has no application on unregistered mortgages, for which the date of creation is everything, produces a contrary result, according priority to A. The date of *creation* (if that is relevant) of his mortgage was clearly anterior to B.'s registration. Thus, the solution urged in Example (iii) produces an anomalous result here. Probably the answer is that section 4 of the Land Charges Act governs; when that section renders A.'s mortgage void against B., it deprives it of the priority it might otherwise expect to collect from its earlier date of creation.

EXAMPLE (v)

Both A. and B. register, A. doing so after the creation of B.'s mortgage but before its registration

Here, chaos is complete. Section 4(5) clearly accords priority to B., for A.'s mortgage was void against him at the time of creation. Section 97 clearly settles the priorities in the order A., B., for that was the order of registration. Clearly, one or other must prevail. The textwriters generally favour the Land Charges Act, which gives the order B., A. Wolstenholme & Cherry favour the Law of Property Act, since it is difficult to see what section 97 is supposed to be doing unless it purports to regulate the question of priority between competing registered mortgages, whereas section 4(5) of the Land Charges Act only applies to a mortgagee by virtue of the definition section (s. 17) which extends the definition of a "purchaser" to include a mortgagee. The suspicion that one section or the other is redundant is confirmed by Example (ii) above. For what it is worth, it is suggested that section 4(5) ought to prevail, for B. may have been induced to lend his money by the fact that there appeared to be no incumbrance, and it is hard to see what further steps B. could have taken to protect himself. A. could easily have protected himself by speedier registration.

(See also Megarry & Wade, *op. cit.*, p. 966; Nokes, p. 88; Cheshire, p. 684; Fisher & Lightwood, p. 425; Waldock, p. 410; Hargreaves [1950] M.L.R. 534).

Even more delightful problems can be invented by assuming the existence of three mortgages. Suppose that mortgages are created in favour of A., B., and C., in that order. A. registers after the creation of B.'s mortgage, but before the creation of C.'s mortgage. Now the answer seems to be:

(a) A. has priority over C. (s. 198).
(b) B. has priority over A. (Land Charges Act, s. 4(5)).
(c) C. has priority over B. (Land Charges Act, s. 4(5)).

In other words, a complete circle has been created. Some authorities attempt to solve the problem by the device of subrogation (see, for example, Megarry & Wade, *op. cit.*, p. 967); but subrogation is essentially an artificial and arbitrary solution, since the whole thing depends upon where one starts to subrogate—in other words, at which point on the circumference of the circle one starts to break in. There is no logical reason for preferring any one point over any other. A more cynical solution might be to supplement the subrogation solution by an action for negligence against his solicitor by the loser in the subrogation lottery, for his solicitor may have failed to register quickly enough. Mr. Lee, in an ingenious article in the *Conveyancer* (1968) 32 Conv. (N.S.) 325 proposes an alternative approach by the theory of equitable charge, which has the merit of taking into account the reasonable expectations of the poor "mortgagees!"

2. Mortgages of Registered Land

Here again, the situation appears to be one of amazing and unnecessary complexity. Although there are only two reported cases on the subject (*Re White Rose Cottage* [1965] Ch. 940

and *Barclays Bank Ltd.* v. *Taylor* [1973] 2 W.L.R. 293) the difficulties surrounding them seem to have been sufficient to release a flood of periodical literature (see, *e.g.* Robinson, [1971] Conv. 100, 168; Ryder, [1966] C.L.P. 26; Jackson, [1972] L.C.R. 476; Baker, [1973] L.Q.R. 170; Hayton, *Registered Land*, pp. 122 *et seq.*). In the present confused state of the authorities, any remarks made here are necessarily tentative.

(a) Registered charges

Here there seems to be an answer. Priority between registered charges is regulated by section 29 of the Land Registration Act 1925, which provided that "subject to any entry to the contrary on the register, registered charges on the same land shall as between themselves rank according to the order in which they are entered on the register, and not according to the order in which they are created."

This section is clearly a close analogy to section 97 of the Law of Property Act, which was considered above, and there is the redeeming feature in this case that there is no section 4(6) of the Land Charges Act 1972 around to complete the confusion. It seems anomalous, though, that a mortgagee who fails to register his charge might prevail over a later chargee by managing to win the registration race—but racing appears to be part of the priority game, at least as far as *Dearle* v. *Hall* (*infra*) is concerned!

There is a problem, as we have seen, as to whether an equitable charge can be registered. The view of Wilberforce J., the trial judge in *White Rose Cottage* in favour of registrability seems to be convincing.

(b) Special mortgage cautions

It seems also that a mortgage protected by *special mortgage caution* (*supra*, p. 16) will rank for priority, from the date of entry of the caution, as if it was a registered charge.

Authority is scanty on the point, as the topic is described

as "obscure" (Cheshire, p. 698) and Ruoff and Roper cheerfully dismiss the whole subject as "expensive, cumbersome, inconvenient, relatively unsafe, and never now used in practice!"

(c) Charges other than registered charges

In *Barclays Bank Ltd.* v. *Taylor* (*supra*) a legal charge, by deed, was created in favour of the bank by the registered proprietor, and the Land Certificate was deposited with the bank. In accordance with standard banking practice, a notice of deposit of the land certificate (*supra*, p. 21) was registered by the bank. Subsequently the registered proprietors contracted to sell the property to the Taylors, who paid over the purchase money without taking a transfer of the land. The Taylors then entered a caution to protect their interest under the estate contract.

At a later stage, the bank sought registration as chargees under section 26, as they wished to exercise their statutory powers, and, as we have seen, substantive registration as a chargee is an essential preliminary to the exercise of a mortgagee's powers where the title to the land is registered (*supra*, p. 15). The Taylors then claimed priority over the bank. It was held by Goulding J. at first instance ([1972] 2 W.L.R. 1038) that the notice of deposit was ineffective to protect the bank's charge; it was a charge by deed, and thus could be protected *only* by a special mortgage caution (s. 106, *supra*, p. 16).

This inconvenient decision was subsequently reversed by the Court of Appeal. The Court of Appeal regarded the issue as a straightforward application of the rule as to priority of equitable interests. The mortgage, they said:

> "albeit taking effect as a minor interest only in equity, did not need any protection against the subsequent equitable interest of the Taylors; it only needed protection against a registration of the Taylors as proprietors (and for this, possession of the land certificate was at least *de facto*

> protection) or against a subsequent mortgagee whose charge was registered or perhaps who lodged a caution in special form (although again here there would, we apprehend, be the same *de facto* protection)."

It is not altogether clear from these remarks whether the "notice of deposit" lodged by the bank was an essential feature of their priority; in view of the court's willingness to apply general equitable principles, the answer is probably in the negative.

In the case of charges protected by caution, the rule seems to be that the charges rank for priority in the order in which the cautions are lodged (*per* Denning M.R., in *White Rose Cottage*, at p. 949). This, however, seems to be subject to the Registrar's discretion under section 55(2) "to make such order as he thinks just" if the caution is warned off and the cautioner appears to defend his interest. It may be assumed that the Registrar and the Court (if the matters came before it) would apply the normal rule of priority of first to register. But what of a prior unregistered mortgage of which the cautioner had notice? Wilberforce J., reviewing some of these problems in *Re White Rose Cottage* (first instance) [1964] Ch. 483, at p. 492, said:

> "These provisions are somewhat perplexing because they give to the Registrar, where a caution is warned, what appears to be a general discretionary power to do what is just without laying down any principle upon which he is to act. One may ask, for example, how he is to deal with a charge having priority in time to that in respect of which the caution had been lodged if that charge has not been protected by registration, notice, or caution, prior to the caution in question, and whether in such a case it is, or is not, relevant to inquire whether or not the cautioner had notice of it."

Mr. Ryder concludes (*loc. cit.*) "No doubt it would be contrary to the general spirit of the Land Registration Act 1925 to hold in circumstances such as this that the earlier charges had priority over the later ones, but it is not easy to see how the reversal of the chronological order of priority could be justified by any specific provision of the Act or Rules." He points out that there is no similar provision to section [4] of the Land Charges Act 1972 making void an unregistered charge against a later incumbrancer.

It is difficult to avoid agreeing with the melancholy verdict of Mr. Hayton that "it is absurd that there is such complexity and obscurity surrounding such everyday matters" ([1972] Conv. 275).

(d) Tacking

Tacking is the process whereby a secured loan gains a higher priority than it would normally achieve under the foregoing rules because the mortgagee is allowed to amalgamate his advance with an earlier mortgage. The archetypal situation where a right to tack might arise is as follows:

(i) A. creates a mortgage in favour of M.1.
(ii) A. creates a later mortgage in favour of M.2.
(iii) A. creates a further mortgage of the same property in favour of M.1.

The question is whether the loan in (iii) can be amalgamated, for priority purposes, to M.1's first mortgage.

"Tacking" takes two forms:

(*i*) *Tabula in naufragio*

As between competing equitable incumbrancers, a doctrine developed that the one who acquired the legal estate first could claim priority. The legal estate was, as it were, the "plank" which enabled the lucky mortgagee to escape from the "shipwreck" of the mortgagor's insolvency and the insufficiency of the security. The doctrine has now been abolished as between competing mortgagees, but may still be relevant as between a mortgagee and other incumbrancer (Law of Property Act s. 94(3)). Thus the doctrine might enable an equitable mortgagee who has acquired the legal estate (*e.g.* under a power of attorney contained in the mortgage) to prevail over a prior equitable incumbrancer such as a purchaser under an estate contract (*McCarthy & Stone* v. *Hodge* [1971] 1 W.L.R. 1547; [1972] C.L.J. 34).

(*ii*) *Further advances*

This form of tacking is much more important. It commonly arises in a situation where a first mortgagee is willing to lend more money to the mortgagor, despite the fact that there has been an intervening mortgage to a second mortgagee. The first mortgagee will be anxious to ensure that his later loan will rank, for purposes of priority, as being on an equal footing with his first loan. The question is of particular importance to banks, who might wish to secure an overdraft which will increase as the mortgagor cashes further cheques on his current account.

The rule is that a further advance may be tacked if (a) the intervening incumbrancer consents or (b) in some circumstances, if the mortgagee had no notice of the intervening incumbrance at the time of his further advance. The meaning of notice in this context varies according to the type of mortgage which is involved. Registration of the intervening incumbrance does not invariably constitute notice to the mortgagee; it would be extremely inconvenient, for instance, if a bank had to conduct a search in the Land Charges Register every time they were asked to cash a cheque by the mortgagor which would increase his overdraft. The question is whether the first mortgage contemplates or obliges a further advance (Law of Property Act s. 94).

(a) No further advance contemplated by the mortgage. Here, normal principles of notice apply; if the advancing mortgagee (M.1.) has actual, constructive, or imputed notice of the second mortgage (M.2.) at the time of his further advance, he will be unable to tack his further advance. If the second mortgage is registered under the Land Charges Act, this will constitute actual notice (Law of Property Act s. 198).

(b) Further advances contemplated, but not obligatory. Here, registration of the intervening mortgage as a land charge does not constitute notice (s. 94(2)). It seems however that if the advancing mortgagee (M.1.) has got notice by some other method, tacking under this head will be prevented (shall not be deemed to have notice of a mortgage by reason *merely* that it was registered as a land charge (s. 94(2)).

(c) Further advance obligatory. If there is an obligation on a mortgagee to make a further advance (*e.g.* upon a bank, which has agreed to honour the cheques of a customer up to an agreed overdraft) it is provided by section 94(1)(*c*) of the Law of Property Act 1925 that neither statutory notice, nor any other kind of notice shall prevent the tacking of a further advance.

Registered land

In the case of registered land, section 94 of the Law of Property Act is excluded (s. 94(4)), and the governing rule is to be found in section 30 of the Land Registration Act. In this case, where the charge contemplates a further advance, the registrar must give notice to the proprietor of the charge of any entry on the register that would prejudicially affect the priority of any further advance made. Until such notice should have reached the chargee, he is not affected by the entry of other charges on the register.

Where the mortgages makes a further advance obligatory, and the obligation is noted on the register, a subsequent registered charge shall take effect subject to any advance which is made in pursuance of the obligation

Mortgages of equitable interests; Dearle v. Hall

It should perhaps be noted that in the case of mortgages of equitable interests in land, a special rule of priority known as the rule in *Dearle* v. *Hall* (1828) 3 Russ. 1 applies. The effect of this rule, the details of which can be found elsewhere (*e.g.* Snell, *Equity*, pp. 71-77) is to make priority depend on the question of which mortgagee first gives notice to the trustees of his incumbrance. The rule was applied to mortgages of equitable interests in land by section 137 of the Law of Property Act 1925.

Note

[1] See also, Megarry and Wade, pp. 951-970; Cheshire, pp. 670-699; Waldock, pp. 381-436; Fisher and Lightwood, pp. 367-437; Nokes, pp. 81-97.

INDEX